Called to Minister... Empowered to Serve

Called to Minister . . . Empowered to Serve

Women in Ministry and Missions in the Church of God Reformation Movement

Edited by Juanita Evans Leonard

Writings by Marie Strong, Sharon Pearson, Susie Stanley, Alice Dise, Nilah Meier-Youngman, Dondeena Caldwell, Ruth M. Smith, June D. Strickland, Vivian Moore, Cheryl Sanders, and Juanita Evans Leonard.

Published by
Warner Press, Inc.
Anderson, Indiana

Copyright ©1989 by Warner Press, Inc.
Anderson, Indiana 46012
International Standard Book Number
0-87162-595-4
All Rights Reserved
Printed in the United States of America
Warner Press, Inc.
Arlo F. Newell, Editor in Chief
Caroline Smith, Editorial Advisor
Dan Harman, Book Editor
Cover by Debbie Apple

In Memory and In Honor of our
Foremothers and to the Daughters
Who Are Called to Minister
and Empowered to Serve

Contents

Chapter   Page

Introduction xiii

1 Biblical Vision:
  An Interpretation of Acts 2:17-18 1
  Marie Strong

2 Biblical Precedence of Women in Ministry 13
  Sharon Pearson

3 Women Evangelists in the Church of God at the
  Beginning of the Twentieth Century 35
  Susie Stanley

4 Black Women in Ministry in the Church of God 57
  Alice Dise

5 Hispanic Women in Ministry in the Church of God....67
  Nilah Meier-Youngman

6 Women in Cross-Cultural Missions of the
  Church of God 81
  Dondeena Caldwell

7 Contemporary Profiles of Women in Ministry 101
  Ruth M. Smith, June D. Strickland,
  and Vivian G. Moore

8 Ethics of Holiness and Unity in the Church of God ...131
  Cheryl Sanders

9 Women, Change, and the Church 149
  Juanita Evans Leonard

Annotated Bibliography 179

Appendix A 165

Appendix B..169

Appendix C 171

Appendix D 177

Annotated Bibliography 179

For Further Reading...............................191

Index 193

This volume is prepared
for the
First Consultation on Women
in Ministry and Missions
of the Church of God Reformation Movement,
June 15, 16, 17, 1989
Sponsored by
The School of Theology of
Anderson University,
Anderson, Indiana.
The book is published
for the Consultation
by
Warner Press, Inc.
Anderson, Indiana

Acknowledgments

It is especially important to acknowledge the many people who have contributed to the writing and compiling of this book. It is difficult albeit dangerous to attempt to list them; even so, the editor must express special thanks

To the men and women of the 1984 Consultation on Mission and Ministry, Directions toward the Year 2000, proceedings under the auspices of the Long-Range Planning Committee of the Executive Council of the Church of God Reformation Movement;

To Jerry Grubbs, Vice-President for Human Services, Anderson University and immediate past Dean of the School of Theology, Anderson University, who kept the dream alive for a Consultation on Women in Ministry, planned and developed for and by women, to explore the results of the 1984 Consultation and the implications for the Church;

To Doris Dale, Executive Secretary of the Women of the Church of God and the 45,000 lay women who provided an initial grant to bring the planning group together;

To the National Steering Committee of the Consultation on Women in Ministry and Missions 1989: Verda Beach, Vivian Raddin Moore, Sharon Pearson, Ann Smith, Ruth Smith, Marie Strong, Cheryl Sanders, June Middlebrooks Strickland, Susie Stanley, and Nilah Meier-Youngman;

To the authors who have given their heart, soul, mind, and strength in developing and writing the essays of this volume;

To Margaret Smith who was selected by the National Steering Committee to assist in the editing of this volume. With her red pencil she has helped direct the compilation of these essays. The time, love and encouragement have bound all the authors together in this testimony of faith.

Acknowledgments

To Caroline Smith, copy editor of Warner Press, whose enthusiasm has shaped the offerings presented into a book worthy of the calling;

To Dan Harman, book editor of Warner Press, who is a man full of energy and encouragement for his sisters as he guided the process of production to its completion;

To Arlo Newell, editor in chief of Warner Press, who was committed to the theological statement made by the authors;

To you, the reader, who will interact with the authors out of your own experience. Thank you for participating with us in this pilgrimage.

Introduction

On the occasion of the first National Consultation on Women in Ministry and Missions of the Church of God Reformation Movement this book is presented in celebration.

This book fills a need for the Reformation Movement that gave birth to it, for the writers who wrote it, and for you who read it. It provides a much needed encouragement to women and men who are engaged in the difficult task of rethinking mission, redesigning curriculum, and redoing theology and ministry within the context of a Holiness community of faith, a community, which has from its beginning in the nineteenth century, affirmed and upheld the place of women in ministry.

Throughout the century-old history of the Reformation Movement, women have given significant leadership as pastors, evangelists, educators, counselors, and cross-cultural workers (missionaries) in North America and in countries around the world. As the twenty-first century approaches, it is fitting to examine the history of some of these women who contributed greatly, not only to this Movement, but to the greater church community.

These women represent the diversity of the Church of God. The biblical foundations for women in ministry will be explored. The role that women have taken in cross-cultural missions of the church will be described. In the chapter devoted to this witness we glimpse how significant the call was and is to those who serve. The relevance of a social ethic to women in ministry will provide the reader with much thought as we look to the twenty-first century. The church must utilize the gifts of ministry that God has given to women and for which they must give an account.

Across America in the late 1970s and 1980s, clergy women of the Church of God began to question the dearth of women clergy in the pulpits of the church. They also raised questions concerning the gifts of women that could be used in the ministries of the church, training institutions, colleges and seminary, and the general program agencies of the church. By far, the most urgent concern was the need for women in the pulpits. In the beginning of the Reformation Movement, women's participation in ministry was not questioned. Now this concern was being voiced by women who held pastorates and were nearing retirement, and by women who had served as minorities in our several colleges, seminary, and agencies. Lay women joined the discussion and prayed for a change in direction.

In the early days of Anderson Bible Training School (1917), now Anderson University, women were studying for the ministry and missions. It seemed imperative in the late 70s and 80s that a few women students and professors at the one seminary of the Church of God should begin to pray, write, and talk about women's call to ministry within the Church of God. To this growing concern the 1984 Consultation on Mission and Ministry: *Directions Toward the Year 2000* under the auspices of the Committee on Long Range Planning of the Executive Council of the Church of God, stated its goals for women and the church. The question was not whether women should have leadership in the church or whether women should be ordained, as many faith communities had debated the issue in the 70s and 80s. For these leaders, the issue was this: "women are being called, trained, and ordained for ministry, but few are being called to local pastorates." (Executive Council Report *2000*, page 9). These leaders said that the church must find the way for the congregations to accept the ministry of women in pastoral and other leadership roles in this generation. An estimated fifty-five percent of the Church of God constituency is comprised of women, and as the life expectancy increases, women will be the majority participants in worship. According to seminary statistics of the past decade, enrollment of women in theological studies is increasing. This book does not consider in depth the nature of all the socio-political factors; however, the authors do point the way to such studies.

Responding to the Consultation of 1984, Anderson University School of Theology accepted the challenge to enable the church by intentionally committing personnel and resources to the goals for women in the whole body of Christ. The Women of the Church of God presented to the seminary an initial gift that facilitated a meeting of eleven clergywomen from different areas of the United States. In St. Louis, Missouri, they gathered for the purpose of exploring the questions raised by the 1984 Consultation. These participants prayed and studied Scripture, shared their ministerial journeys, dreamed and designed the first Consultation on Women in Ministry and Mission, and outlined this book. The Consultation and the book have the advantage of having been conceived out of the collective journey of women in the Church of God ministry/missions.

The authors of this book have known the call to ministry/missions; they have known rejection and triumph; they have known persecution and fulfillment. Above all, the authors say to those who read this volume that there is a history, that there is a story set in motion by the biblical writers and empowered by the Holy Spirit for today and for the next generations. The hope of the authors is that the story we have told will help you, the reader, to be encouraged for the ministry to which God has called you. This book is but a reflection of what has been and what is. The action is still in process. A full history of the women who have given their lives in ministry throughout the first hundred years of the Reformation Movement is yet to be written. The changing role of women in society and its effect upon the role of women within the church must be explored elsewhere.

Our foremothers have woven a tapestry with a rich pattern. They have passed it on to us in this generation. It is our prayer that the threads we add will encourage and challenge women and men to serve God and all humanity through the power of the Holy Spirit.

Juanita Evans Leonard
Associate Professor, Church and Society
School of Theology, Anderson University
Coordinator of National Consultation on
Women in Ministry and Mission

Marie Strong

Dr. Marie Strong is Professor Emerita of Anderson University. She taught at Anderson University for thirty-three years in Religion. She is an ordained minister of the Church of God and has pastored congregations in Nebraska.

During her teaching career at Anderson University she was involved in planning programs for Christian witness. She was founder of the service organization for students known as Christianity in Action. She also helped found the Anderson Christian Center, a rehabilitation center for alcoholics and prisoners.

She has authored two books and many articles for Colloquium, Vital Christianity, Christian Leadership, Church of God Missions, *and* Pathways to God. *She has written Church School curriculum materials and programs for* Women of the Church of God.

A frequent guest speaker for ministers' conventions and Women of the Church of God retreats, she has served as guest lecturer for college classes and for seminars.

Chapter 1:

The Biblical Vision
An Interpretation of Acts 2:17-18
Marie Strong

Introduction

An honest Bible student cannot give the meaning of a
scripture out of context. I am therefore compelled to explain
something about prophecy, and in particular, the prophecy
of Joel that was quoted by Peter in chapter two of Acts.

Background

Acts, Chapter 1

Acts begins with the facts that Jesus had died, been
buried, and was resurrected. Luke is the only writer who
records the account of Jesus spending forty days with his
disciples after the Resurrection (Acts 1:3).

It is during the forty days of teaching that Jesus asked his disciples to remain in the city of Jerusalem and wait for the promise of the Father or the Baptism of the Holy Spirit (vv. 4, 5). "You shall receive power" he said, "when the Holy Spirit has come upon you, and you shall be my witnesses in Jerusalem, and in all Judea and Samaria and to the end of the earth" (Acts 1:8). After saying this, Jesus ascended into heaven.

The disciples returned to Jerusalem and waited. Included in the waiting group were the Apostles, women, Mary the mother of Jesus, and the brothers of Jesus (v. 14). There were one hundred twenty of them (v. 15).

The Setting of the Scripture

Acts 2:17-18

The time of the event is the Day of Pentecost. Pentecost was a very important religious festival celebrating the giving of the Law on Mount Sinai. It came fifty days after the Passover. Passover was a festival celebrating the Jews' departure from Egypt when God saved the Jewish people from Egyptian bondage. Jesus was killed during the Passover season.

Jewish festivals were very important to the retention of Jewish faith. Travel was comparatively easy in the first century because Rome controlled all of the Mid-East from Spain on the west to the Caspian Sea and the Persian Gulf on the east; from southern Europe and northern Africa, it included all of the area known as the Middle East today. Because Rome controlled the entire Mediterranean world, no visas or passports were necessary. Good Roman roads, constructed for the benefit of the Roman army and the governmental system, made traveling very easy. Traveling was relatively safe because Roman troops patrolled the roads and their legions protected their cities. The Jews took advantage of all of this, and each Jewish male hoped to go to Jerusalem and attend one of the Jewish festivals at least once during his lifetime.

At the particular Pentecost mentioned in Acts 2, Jews

came from more than a dozen areas of the Roman Empire (Acts 2:8-11). One of the miracles of that particular Pentecost was that of language. Those Jews coming from areas representing a dozen different languages heard those languages being used by ignorant fishermen. That is, those from Egypt apparently heard in Coptic and those from Rome heard Latin, and so forth. The average Jewish man was not ignorant. He had been taught in the synagogue school and could read and write in Aramaic. Since most were merchants and the language of commerce at the time was Greek, he probably could also understand Greek. The Apostles at Pentecost could have spoken in Aramaic and been understood by all. Through the power of the Holy Spirit, who had recently come upon them, the Apostles were able to speak in other languages. It was a miracle, and all present probably recognized it as such. It is no wonder that the Jewish visitors were amazed and asked, "What does this mean?" (v. 12). As in nearly every crowd, there were some who ridiculed the event and said, "They are drunk" (v. 13). Peter immediately let the crowd know that they were not drunk. This, Peter said, "is what was spoken by the prophet Joel" (vv. 15-16).

Joel is not well-known among modern Christians. Possibly some do not even know the book is in the Bible. Joel, possibly more than any other prophet, laid the groundwork for the activity of the church as it is depicted in the first few chapters of the book of Acts. Paul's theology of Christian freedom has much in common with the prophecy of Joel.

The Prophet Joel

We need to look closely at the writing of Joel for two reasons: First, within this small book is the major statement regarding women in ministry that was held by the first century church from its beginning. Second, Joel took a position of "thus saith the Lord" about a fact as simple as an agricultural crisis. He spoke to the current situation. If Joel were alive today he would probably have a message from God about poverty, the environment, drugs, or other social problems that plague our world.

3

Joel, as all prophets before him, spoke to the current situation, which was an agricultural crisis. The land was being devastated by locusts. There are many kinds of locusts, and the Hebrew language has used seven different terms to describe them. Joel uses four terms. He uses a poetic style of writing and possibly used the four different terms to show the "completeness of the destruction" (Smith 1911, 74, 75). Note how Joel does this:

What the cutting locust left,
The swarming locust has eaten.
What the swarming locust left,
The hopping locust has eaten.
And what the hopping locust left,
The destroying locust has eaten.—Joel 1:4

Joel notes that before this no one had ever seen or heard of such destruction. The plague of locusts apparently came just before the grape harvest, so that the "drunkards weep" because there will be no wine (v. 5). There will be no offerings because the fields of grain "are laid waste" (1:9-10). The wheat, barley, and all the fruit from the fruit trees were destroyed. The animals "are perplexed because there is no pasture for them" (1:19). Even wild animals cry because "the water brooks are dried up." The "seed shrivels under the clods" (1:17). This last phrase, Thompson says, "occurs no where else in the Old Testament" (Thompson 1956, 742).

To Joel all of this is a picture of the "day of the Lord" which to Joel and to most prophets was a "terrible day" (2:1). The locusts are "Yahweh's army" (2:11, 25). "Yet even now," says the Lord, "return to me with all your heart . . . return to the Lord. . . . Who knows whether he will not turn and repent and leave a blessing behind him" (2:12-14).

Joel imagines the people repent (or they actually do repent) because of the judgment of God in sending the locusts, and prosperity returns. The fields are green again (2:22). Rain has come (2:23). There is abundant grain, and people will eat and be satisfied (2:24-26). "Then Israel will know that I (God) am in the midst of Israel" (9:27).

The Coming of the Holy Spirit

It shall come to pass afterward: after the time of material prosperity (2:28).

I will pour out my Spirit: The words *pour out* in Joel 2:28 and Acts 2:27 show the abundance of the gift.

Upon all flesh: Because of the context, most scholars believe that Joel meant all in Israel, not all other nations, for the other nations are pictured as destroyed in Joel 3:2, 9ff. (See also Lanchester 1915, 66; Watts 1975, 39; and Smith 1911, 123.) This may have been Joel's intention, because he, as well as other Jews, could not foresee a Gentile mission. Peter, quoting this scripture on the day of Pentecost (Acts 2:17) may also have this limited view of Jewish exclusiveness. Peter finally sees the true meaning of the Spirit's coming, but only after having a special vision of a sheet coming down from heaven full of unclean animals, being told to kill and eat, and being informed that what God has cleansed is not to be called unclean. Only after the vision appears three times was Peter willing to go and preach to the Roman Cornelius (Acts 10). It took the Jewish Christian church sometime before they realized that Jesus died for all of humankind and not only for the Jewish people (Acts 11:18 and Gal. 3:8). Any person, not only special prophets, can understand and disseminate spiritual truth.

Joel gives examples of this broad meaning: *Your sons and your daughters shall prophesy* (Acts 2:17). Prophesy means to understand divine truth and feel inspired to tell it. *Sons* in a patriarchal society, could not make any decision without the consent of the oldest male in the family or tribe. For Joel to suggest that sons would prophesy must have sounded very radical. It must have been exciting news to the young men.

The words of Joel, *your daughters shall prophesy,* were radical in the extreme. In most cultures women have held a very low position for hundreds of years. Aristotle said that woman had a natural deficiency. She was on a lower level than man. In contrast a recent Hebrew writer says that the Jewish

Jewish gifts not
taught in the
Synagogue

mother is "ruler of the household, the dominant figure of influence and love" (Brayer 1986 Vol. II). Is this true? And what is meant by "ruler of the household"?

The Jewish View of Woman

In the Old Testament creation story, woman was taken from man's side, which may have meant she had more equality than later history gave her. According to Georgia Harkness, woman was property listed along with the cattle (Harkness 1972, 42-52). Just where the Hebrew male got his his low view of woman is not certain.

Even Brayer admits to a contrast between the treatment of female babies from that of male ones. There is much rejoicing, he says, at the birth of a son, with relatives and friends bringing in food and doing household chores. There are formal religious ceremonies both at the bedside at the time of birth and for each stage of the child's development. The father holds the young boy child on his lap and teaches him. The young boy is taught in the synagogue schools and later educated in more formal ways. The girl child, by contrast, received her name in the synagogue with a special prayer (Brayer 1986 Vol. II, 37-42). Previous to the Christian era. girls were not taught in the synagogue schools. They were taught domestic and wifely duties by their mothers.

The Jewish mother appeared to be "ruler of the home" in the sense that she cooked and cleaned and cared for the children. In modern times she might also be in charge of a small business belonging to her husband while he studied the Torah.

Brayer admits that "every morning the Jewish male pronounces the following blessing, 'blessed art thou, Lord, our God, King of the universe, who has not made me a woman.' " The author insists that the man is grateful that he has been saved from the pain of childbirth and caring for the home and is therefore free to study the Torah. Brayer says that the women thank God that they have not been born male and are therefore free from the bondage of study of the Torah (Brayer 1986 Vol. II, 208).

worth if womens life —
limited

The story of perhaps the lowest treatment of women is in Judges 19:16—21:24. Gang rape of a woman is considered more acceptable than a homosexual relationship among men. The young woman's body (she died from the sexual assault) was cut up and sent to all of the tribes. Since the tribe of Benjamin was guilty, the other tribes swore an oath not to give their daughters to that tribe. Virgins were taken in war and others were kidnapped to supply the men of Benjamin with wives. The story is too long and involved to relate here. It is gruesome and we hope not typical of Hebrew life. It is not the first time that a woman's life is found to be less important than a sworn oath or producing male heirs. See *e.g.* the story of Judah in Genesis 38:12-26 or the story of Jephthah in Judges 11:30, 34-39. Harkness reminds us that

> faithfulness in the marriage bond did not weigh heavily with husbands . . . that Samson visited a harlot at Gaza and appears to have suffered no blame. . . . David's sin with Bathsheba is condemned indeed, but the ground of condemnation is the wrong done to her husband and not any wrong to Bathsheba (Harkness 1972, 48).

Women Models in the Old Testament: The Prophetess

Because of the low position of women generally and the authoritarian attitude of husbands toward wives, there are few Old Testament examples of women leaders in the literature.

The first woman called "prophetess" in the Old Testament is Miriam, sister of Moses (Exodus 15:20), who sang the song of triumph at the Red Sea. Her later history wasn't as commendable. Miriam and her brother Aaron protested Moses's marriage to the Cushite woman and apparently started a revolt of Moses's leadership (Numbers 12). For this action Miriam was stricken with leprosy and lost favor by being put outside the camp for seven days.

One cannot prove race prejudice in this case, but there is a strong impression of it. Was Aaron's and Miriam's anger with Moses because he had married the black woman or was there some other unknown cause?

No such reflection is cast on the prophetess Deborah who merits two entire chapters in the book of Judges (Chapters 4 and 5). Deborah was already known as a prophetess in Israel and a charismatic (God gifted) judge before she led the army. She led in battle only because she was forced by circumstances to do so. The general of the army, Barak, was a coward and refused to lead unless Deborah went with him. The writer of the account says that because of Barak's cowardice the credit for the military success will go to a woman. The woman, Jael, in the story, is credited with killing the Canaanite general by driving a tent pin through his head. A further insult to Barak was the fact that Jael was a foreigner.

Instrumental in the religious revival under King Josiah was Huldah, the prophetess. She fulfilled both prophetic requirements. She fearlessly gave the word of the Lord and the news was bad. When King Josiah asked the priest to "go inquire of the Lord," the priest went immediately to Huldah, the prophetess. It is unfortunate that all that is known of Huldah is this one incident found in 2 Kings 22:14-20 and the parallel passage in 2 Chronicles 34:19-28.

Georgia Harkness reminds us of the prophetess Noadiah who merits only one phrase in the book of Nehemiah (6:14). Harkness wishes we knew more about Noadiah, and says, "a woman important enough to frighten Nehemiah or at least make him mention her as an opponent? There must be a story behind that" (Harkness 1972, 45-46).

There is a prophetess who appears at the dedication ceremony of the baby Jesus. Although mentioned only in the New Testament (Luke 2:36-38) Anna seems to be of the Old Testament type. She lived at the temple and prayed day and night. She was one of the few who recognized Jesus, thus placing her within the range of God's voice or revelation. There were possibly other Jewish women prophetesses in Hebrew life who never made it into the literature.

The Jewish people today honor Esther. Esther is not called a prophetess. She cannot be seen so much in that role as in the role of the faithful wife fearlessly influencing her husband.

Joel defends the spiritual rights of slaves in the passage quoted in Acts 2:18: *on my menservants and my maidservants, . . . I will pour out my Spirit and they shall prophesy.* Even the slaves, male and female, can receive divine truth and feel divinely led to share it. The gospel was meant for all people everywhere. There is in Joel's prophecy, quoted by Peter, no race discrimination, no religious descrimination, and no age or sex prejudice. God may call anyone to be the voice to the time. That message has eternal significance. We should listen. To reject any prophet or minister of God because of race, culture, age, or sex is to reject God.

Conclusion

no racial or sexist descrimination

The first century church had no problem with the section of Joel's prophecy regarding women in ministry. They did have a problem with Gentile inclusion but soon passed that barrier.

From the beginning of his Christian experience Paul had the Joel prophecy in his heart, possibly by divine revelation. He was not only the apostle to the Gentiles but accepted women in ministry as part of the gospel message which is best expressed in Galatians 3:28:

> There is neither Jew nor Greek,
> there is neither slave nor free,
> there is neither male nor female;
> for you are all one in Christ Jesus.

Paul continually lived this out in his ministry. There were Phoebe (Rom. 16:1), Priscilla, the teacher of the great Christian orator Apollos (Acts 18:26), there were Euodia and Syntyche, pastors in Philippi (Phil. 4:2ff.); there was Apphia in the address to Philemon and Nympha (Col. 4:15) and nine women mentioned in the twenty-eight names listed as fellow workers in Romans 16.

Women, we are a part of a great tradition. We are called to minister in many areas of human need. Feminine voices are needed in all of the troubled areas of our world. If Joel was concerned about locusts, we should be concerned about world peace, drugs, health, the environment, poverty, and other problems. We, after all, are the ones held responsible for the food on our tables. Mothers, more than fathers, seem to suffer when their young men are sent to battlefields. (Fathers, in our culture, are taught to glorify war.) In whatever area of ministry God calls us, we must fulfill the prophetic role, *i.e.* speak the word of God to the current issues and give the timeless message of salvation to all.

If we are selected as part of a concerned group on committees or boards, we must get God's message and speak. The feminine voice is needed. If it is given with feminine dignity and humility, it might yet save the world from extinction.

If God gives a message we need confidence to speak or act. Complete dependence upon God results in a perfect balance of humility and confidence; humility because we know that we, ourselves, do not have the answers; and confidence because we know that God does.

There are some very positive scriptures to help us. Among them is 1 Cor. 1:26-30 where ordinary people had convinced the people of influence, and where people without worldly wisdom had convinced the wise; and where weak and powerless people had convinced the strong. Concluding these remarks Paul said:

> [God] is the source of your life in Christ Jesus, whom God made our wisdom, our righteousness and sanctification and redemption.

So be encouraged, women. The battle is not ours, but God's. God will supply what is needed to win. The following scripture is designed for harmonious work in the church. Paul knew that the power of God is love, and said:

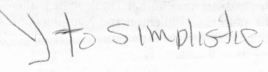

10

Love one another with [sisterly] affection; outdo one another in showing honor; never be lacking in zeal, be aglow with the spirit, serve the Lord. Practice hospitality. . . . Live in harmony with one another. . . . Be careful to do what is right in the eyes of everybody. If it is possible, as far as it depends on you, live in peace with everyone. . . . Do not be overcome by evil, but overcome evil with good.

(Taken from Rom. 12:9-21, using RSV and NIV as sources.)

Sharon Clark Pearson

Sharon Pearson is an ordained minister serving in Long Beach, California. She is a candidate for the Ph.D. degree at Fuller Theological Seminary in New Testament Studies.

Her writings have been published in Vital Christianity, Reach magazine, Between Times *magazine,* Pathways to God, Concern, *and the* Peace Fellowship Newsletter. *She has written Adult Bible Curriculum materials and program materials for Women of the Church of God.*

Sharon has been an instructor in Biblical Studies at Anderson University and at Azusa Pacific University. She is a consultant for Infant Care programs and has served as counselor and therapist in most aspects of local pastoral ministry.

Chapter 2:

Biblical Precedents for Women in Ministry

Sharon Pearson

The Church of God historically has held a "high view" of Scripture. The Bible has been accepted as the authority of faith and life in the Church. For a church that claims the integrity and authority of Scripture, questions of practice are taken seriously. An early motto "The Bible is our creed" is a classical expression of that conviction. This motto assumes that it is possible to be directed by Scripture. It also refuses any attempt to define the revelation contained in Scripture in any "manmade creed." This refusal is one of high principle and a certain wisdom, and yet is a source of anxiety for many in the church, for in it are the seeds of diversity. Yet, most in the church, at least those who are thoughtful, are willing to live within the tension of a unity born only of the fellowship of salvation.

It must be stated at the beginning of this chapter that a certain tension also is apparent in Scripture. There is a tension between the eschatological vision (end times) of the prophet Joel as quoted on the Day of Pentecost (Acts) and statements based upon propriety and convention. Arguments of hierarchy and dominance/subordination stand alongside stories of revolutionary attitudes and practice in Jesus' ministry and in the participation of women in ministry of the early church.

Because of the high value the Church traditionally has placed upon Scripture, it is important in our church culture to talk about 'biblical precedents' when discussing questions not explicitly defined in Scripture. A common commitment to Scripture is certainly a part of the ethos of our community.

To determine biblical precedents requires careful study. All serious (and even not-so-serious) Bible students interpret Scripture according to some set of principles. When any question is asked of Scripture, certain principles are exercised in the selection, evaluation (valuing), theological synthesis of those materials, and proposed application of those conclusions. For the question of Women in Ministry, interpretation is crucial to women because their personal/relational lives and their participation in the Church has been defined and regulated largely by the use of Scripture.

All who read Scripture make choices between the instructions received therein. All decide what portion of the Scripture is timeless and always applicable and those cultural expressions of some larger question. For example, though many have read the Apostle Paul's instructions that women wear veils in public worship, there is no concern expressed in the Church of God that this injunction is to be obeyed by women today. It has been dismissed as time (circumstance) bound instruction that no longer applies. The question then, is not whether to make such distinctions (which are in fact demanded by the nature of many of the texts in the New Testament—occasional letters), but where to draw the line in that process. In making a choice I am governed by two almost automatic instincts as I write. First, I believe that we are allowed to define an expression as limited to a particular circumstance (with a corresponding application) when we have a clear statement of such limits from that text or another. Second, an old dictum applies: Where the text speaks, we speak (without reservation). Where Scripture is silent, we speak only with a great deal of humility. ⁓TᴜᴜR

Some of the questions we address to the Scripture are foreign to it. These may be worked out only by implication. The question this chapter addresses is not foreign to the New Testament but is not answered explicitly. While it is clear that women participated in the ministry of the early church, there are no texts that clearly define women's participation in ministry according to office and authority. Therefore, all who address this question to the New Testament must work by implication. In that case, it is necessary to review the information on women in general in the New Testament.

It has already been noted that the Scripture was written, selected, and preserved in an androcentric (man-centered) society. It is remarkable that given its patriarchal world-view, women were included in the story at all. An abundance of evidence is available in the various accounts of women in the New Testament, however, indicating that women were an integral part of the life of the Church.

Women in the Gospels

It is impossible to consider the place of women in the church without recalling Jesus' attitude and actions toward the women around him. Women as well as men were attracted to Jesus in his three short years of ministry. Among Jesus' rugged band of followers were a number of women. Jeremias calls this event "an unprecedented happening in history of that time" (Jeremias 1949, 374). We know about these women from a few short references (Mark 15:40-41; Luke 8:1-3). Record holds that these women supported Jesus and his disciples financially. They were women with means and so probably from an upper echelon of society. The Marcan account paints the poignant picture of these

15

women along with other women from Jerusalem at the scene of Jesus' crucifixion. The three women named in that portrait visit the burial site after Sabbath to anoint their Lord's body for burial. And then, in a society where a woman's word was not allowed in court, they were commissioned by Jesus to be the first to proclaim the Resurrection. Nothing was more natural than their being among the 120 who waited in the Upper Room for the power that would give fire to their lives and witness. The Church from its inception included women.

Who were the women who sought out Jesus and became a part of the gospel story because of his impact upon their lives? They were the three who became known as leaders among the group of women (Mary Magdalene, Mary the mother of Joses, and Salome). They were Mary and Martha, who contrary to social rules invited Jesus into their home. They included the woman unclean with her feminine infirmity and the Samaritan woman at the well. They were the Syrophonecian (Gentile) woman who asked him for "the crumbs" for her demon-possessed daughter and the woman who anointed his feet.

The significant aspect of every story is that it was ever recorded and preserved. In a culture where women were property and had no rights or privileges to call their own, these stories themselves would have opened the door of the church to criticism and contempt. Furthermore, in every case, the import of the story is that Jesus crossed all lines of propriety—religious and social. His very actions were a challenge to the cherished traditions of his own people. He went so far as to commend women as examples of faith and spiritual vitality, women who were not counted in the number of a synagogue, who were isolated to a separate court at the Temple, and whose religious vows could be overturned by their husbands.

Just as significant as the story of the women who accompanied Jesus and his disciples is the story of Mary and Martha. Jesus teaches Mary as he would teach any man who would follow him—an unheard of breach of religious leadership. "Better to burn the Torah than to teach it to a woman"

(Jeremias 1949, 373). Women were not educated in the Synagogue school nor at home. "He who teaches his daughter the law, teaches her lechery" (Jeremias 1949, 373). As if that were not enough Jesus is recorded as having chided Martha for fulfilling her socially prescribed role instead of joining Mary (Luke 10:38-42).

The cumulative effect of these stories is that Jesus broke custom in his championing of women as equally worthy of his concern and ministry. His evaluation of them far outstripped the most expansive and tolerant in his day and continually surprised even those who knew him well. The tone of his ministry was not to accept the status quo, but rather to model a new life and relationships for women. He challenged the sexist standards of his world—the lustful glance of an adulterous heart (Matthew 5:27-32), the casual divorce, a male prerogative (Matthew 19:3-9. See Jeremias 1949, 370), or the threat of the most fearful punishment applied unfairly—only to the adulterous woman (John 8:1-11. The popular attitude of the day was that women were responsible for all sexual temptation and therefore sexual sin.) None of these stories would be approved, much less applauded outside of the early church that preserved them. Yet, somehow, the Gospel could not be told without them. Such events were so integral to the reality of the Jesus community that they comprised a part of the gospel.

An anticipated response to the previous display of evidence in consideration of the question of women in ministry is the popular objection that none of the women following Jesus became one of the disciples. None of the apostles were women. None were accorded equality. It is not necessary to argue cultural expediency here. It is enough to respond that no Gentile or slave was allowed that privilege either, but that was not and is not used to exclude these disadvantaged groups in the leadership and offices of the church.

Women in the Early Church

Clearly women were an integral part of the Jesus community that awaited the empowerment of the Spirit (Acts 1:14-

15). And just as clearly these women were among those who received the Spirit in fulfillment of Joel's prophecy (Acts 2:1-4). In the same way that it was incredible that the stories of women were incorporated into the Gospel accounts, it is also a wonder that participation of women in the early church was recorded in Acts and the Epistles. Against all cultural expediency and propriety, the story continues to be told. A brief perusal of the evidence of this participation, culled by many others can be listed in two categories: (1) brief references included in such incidental fashions as lists of women, and (2) epistolatory discussions of women's participation in ministry.

I. Lists of Women

One type of evidence in the New Testament that will be considered is the brief references to women identified as participating in various aspects of the ministry of the church. Phillip the evangelist is noted not for his own gift and ministry, but rather for his four daughters who had the gift of prophesy, (which by the Apostle Paul's estimation was the highest gift). Priscilla, listed in several epistles in the New Testament, evidently bore quite a reputation. (Acts 18:2, 18, 26; 1 Corinthians 16:19; Romans 16:3-4; 2 Timothy 4:19—how many others were referred to as often or in such a variety of texts?) Her distinction here is that she, along with Aquila taught Apollos (Acts 18:26). Against rabbinic tradition that identified women only as "the wife" of the man who is named, the Apostle Paul recognized Priscilla as prominent enough not only to be listed along with her husband, but also to be referred to first in the pair more often than not (four of six times). By calling Priscilla a "fellow worker" in Christ Jesus, the Apostle Paul accorded Priscilla as well as Aquila, an equal place among other such workers as Timothy (Romans 16:21), Titus (2 Cor. 8:23), Luke (Philemon 24), Apollos and Paul (1 Cor. 3:9) and others.

This term applied to Priscilla was also applied to Euodia and Syntyche, leaders at Philippi. Phoebe is called a "minister" (historically translated as 'servant' only in the case of Phoebe). The same term was applied to the leaders Apollos (1 Cor. 3:5), Timothy (1 Tim. 4:6), and Paul (1 Cor. 3:5). Four women are listed in the closing instructions of Paul's letter to the Romans as having "worked very hard" in the Lord: Mary, Tryophena, Tryphosa, and Persis. The Apostle Paul applied that same description to the ministry of other leaders in the Church (1 Cor. 16:15-16; 1 Thess. 5:12; 1 Tim. 5:17).

Finally, it is probable that the reference in Romans 16:7 to two who were "outstanding among the apostles" included a woman. The name in question is Junias. David Scholer's review of the evidence is most helpful:

> Junias is a male name in English translations, but there is no evidence that such a male name existed in the first century A.D. Junia, a female name, was common, however. The Greek grammar of the sentence . . . means that the male and female forms of this name would be spelled identically. . . . Since Junia is the name attested in the first century and since the great church father . . . of the fourth century, John Chystostom (no friend of women in history), understood the reference to be to a woman Junia, we ought to see it that way as well. In fact, it was not until the thirteenth century that she was changed to Junias (Scholer 1984, 12-13).

It is obvious from these informal, uncontrived lists that women played a significant role in the early church as leaders. Their function in ministry is defined in those places by the same terms applied to the ministry of men without distinction in role or function. It is also clear that both the actual ministry and the record of that ministry were more limited for women than for men.

II. Evidence of Participation

One of the strongest evidences for the participation of women in the worshiping community comes from the brief discussion of 1 Corinthians 11:2-16. This text makes explicit reference to women prophesying and praying in services of worship. The reference is incidental; the practice is not commented upon. Such participation by women is evidently assumed under the wide rubric of spiritual gifts and ministries that have been designated to all (regardless of religious, social, or sexual distinctions) for "the common good" (12:7).

Verse three makes one of the basic assertions referred to often in the discussion of women in ministry: "Now, I want you to realize that the head of every man is Christ, and the head of the woman is man, and the head of Christ is God." While it seems obvious that the Apostle Paul is appealing to some sort of order here, the meaning and application of the statement is much less obvious. This statement is made in service of Paul's argument that women ought not abandon headcoverings in their exercise of ministry (public prayer and prophecy). Whatever his statement does mean, it in no way functions in this text to limit the participation or leadership of women in public worship. It is meant rather to maintain the "natural" traditions of headcoverings (and the meaning of those headcoverings).

The term *head* is most often translated elsewhere as "origin" or "source." Translated by these terms makes quite a different statement than "head" when understood as "lord." If translated as "lord," this passage could be used to promote the idolatry of men by women; women would owe men what men owe Christ. While Paul is appealing to the order of creation from Genesis 2:18-23, he does not go so far as a straight parallel would allow. He does not claim that woman is the *image* as well as glory of man (1 Cor. 11:7). Woman, too, shares the image of God (and therefore is not more removed from God than man); Paul concedes this to Genesis 1:27 and 5:2 (Barrett 1968, 248-249). Verse eight restates the concept of "origin" or "source" in the order of creation. It may be that "priority" includes a sense of superiority here, but that meaning is not supported by the text in Genesis. (See discussion under "Argument from Creation Accounts")

Paul makes a summary statement in verse ten: "For this reason and because of the angels, the woman ought to have

women too share the image 20 of God

a sign of authority on her head" (NIV). The translation of this text is misleading. The Greek term *authority* should be translated as it is—that woman should have "authority" on her head. It is not to be translated to "sign of authority" or "veil" on her head (Scholer 1984, 17). The angels here are to be understood as guardians of the created order who are not to be offended by oversight of this principle of sexual differentiation. The veil now not only symbolizes woman's glorification of man but also her authority to play an active role in worship. "That is, her veil represents the new authority given to women under the new dispensation to do things which formerly had not been permitted" (Barrett 1968, 255). This interpretation is substantiated by the two verses following his statement. Having argued for natural differences between man and woman, Paul now lays down a new principle of mutuality and interdependence based also upon creation (cf. 1 Cor. 7:3-5).

A question is raised when the words of 1 Corinthians 14:33-36 confront us. They seem to limit the role of women in worship only three chapters after women are casually recognized for their participation and leadership. The apparent discontinuity between these two passages has been explained in a variety of ways (Martin 1984, 84-88). But no matter what final conclusion one places upon these words, it cannot be that women are not allowed to participate in public worship. Ralph Martin's argument is basic:

> Paul remains committed to social egalitarianism in the gospel (Gal. 3:28), and there is the undeniable evidence of the role he accorded women colleagues (Phoebe, Prisca [Priscilla], the women of Philippi [Phil. 4:3, sic.] and the several coworkers in Rom. 16). It is *prima facie* unlikely he should state categorically "Let your women keep silent" in worship (Martin 1984, 85).

The best solution, which gives fair consideration to all of the evidence in this case, is to recognize the special use of the verb *speak (lalein)* as "inspired speech." The picture drawn by the text and by the larger context of this epistle is of women who aspired to be charismatic teachers, claiming special revelations in inspired speech that were above the usual corrections of the congregation and apostolic teaching. Their claims were so inflated that the apostle is lead to sarcasm: "Did the word of God originate with you? Or are you the only people it has reached?"

The heretical teaching going on in the Corinthian congregations was, in fact, agnostic teaching (cf. ch. 7 and 15). These women sharing in a claim of "special knowledge," which included speculations that there was no actual resurrection of the body but that a spiritual "resurrection" had already occurred at baptism. They prompted Paul's extended reply beginning with his question, "How can some of you say that there is no resurrection of the dead?" (15:12) Their denial of the resurrection lay in their claim to be raised at baptism—they were "angelic beings" (13:1) after a misapplication of the words of Jesus in Luke 20:35-36. Such a concept lead to a confusion in the home; as resurrected beings they no longer participated in marriage obligations—they were attempting to live in a state of celibacy in marriage (7:3-5).

These heretical teachers (women glossolalics) were to be kept "under control" as the "law" required (*nomos*, meaning "principle," and here referring to Paul's teaching; cf. vs. 37). The meaning of "asking their husbands at home" is a response to the challenge these women presented to their husbands in public assembly. The verb "inquire after" (*eperotan*) is used in the sense of interrogation, in the same way as they challenged apostolic authority. This interpretation, offered by Martin, fits the larger portrait drawn of the women in the Corinthian church. These women were abusive of their new found freedoms. They discarded their veils (11:5) and practiced a negative spirituality full of pride and competition. This portrait, drawn carefully by Martin (Martin 1984, 86-88), is supported by a parallel circumstance in 1 Timothy 2:8-15 where arrogant women have aspired to be teachers of things they know not (possibly also teaching agnostic perspectives).

The above discussions of the participation of women in public worship and lists of women who lead in the early church all bear evidence to the fact that women did function in ministry in the early church. While there is no claim to "office" here, there is no question but that "function" occurred.

The Use of Household Codes

One significant aspect of the argument against women in ministry is the appeal to the household codes located in the New Testament. These household codes were not created by the New Testament authors but rather are quoted from the Graeco-Roman culture of that day (Elliott 1981 and Balch 1981). The Greek philosopher Aristotle, who predated Christ by three and a half centuries, was the source of the formal arrangement of pairings based on the dominant/subordinate hierarchical model:

> The primary and smallest parts of the household are master and slave, husband and wife, father and children. . . . Authority and subordination are conditions—not only inevitable but also expedient. . . . There is always found a ruling and a subject factor . . . between the sexes, the male is by nature superior and the female inferior, the male ruler and the female subject (Aristotle 1932).

Aristotle expanded this household code to the realm of political life because in his thinking, "the household was a microcosm of the state" (Balch 1984, 161-3). He taught the authority/subordination model in the pairing of ruler/people. He promoted his social order as necessary to stability, harmony, and political security.

Any threat to this Aristotelian value system was considered by the Roman Empire to be a threat to such stability and security. So, the Roman emperor Octavian instructed his soldiers to "allow no woman to make herself equal to a man" (Casius 1917). What was the occasion for such a concern? Anthony and Cleopatra. David Balch reviews the problem as follows:

If democratic equality between husband and wife as it existed in Egypt were allowed to influence Roman households, the government would degenerate into a democracy; and the Romans believed this changed form of government would be morally worse than the aristocracy or monarchy which had brought them to power. The Egyptian Cleopatra's goddess Isis, who "gave women the same power as men" was perceived as a threat to continued Roman rule (Cassius 1917, 162-3).

The rights of the one in authority were assumed. Tyranny was not criticized as an expression of that authority in the dominant culture as directed by Aristotle's words: "For there is no such thing as injustice in the absolute sense towards what is one's own" (Aristotle 1956).

This lengthy look back is necessary for us to recover the impact of the household codes as used in the New Testament. The impact is not that the Roman household codes were simply adopted but rather that they were *qualified* in the earlier New Testament texts (in chronological order—Col. 3:18—4:1; Eph. 5:21-6:9, 1 Pet. 2:13—3:7). They were not accepted as absolutes, but critiqued even as they were appealed to. For example, in Colossians 3:18—4:1, the traditional pairings are each followed by an unthinkable modification, which in fact, points to a higher code of ethics than the one encapsulated in the original codes:

> wives be subject to husbands _____ husbands love wives
> children obey parents _____ fathers do not provoke children
> slaves obey masters _____ masters treat slaves justly (Balch 1984, 161).

The injunctions of the code in Ephesians are filled with new meaning as they appear under the paragraph heading "submit to one another" which is applied to all of the following discussion. The reason given here is not an appeal to the superior or inferior nature of the other, but rather, reverence to Christ. It is impossible for the twentieth century student of the Bible to appreciate fully the newness of the relationship commanded of husbands and wives in Ephesians. Likewise, the command to Christian masters was full of the seeds of change: "treat your slaves in the same way" (i.e. by the same set of attitudes and conduct required of Christian slaves). Such radical qualifications of the household codes are a class apart from any parallel in Greek philosophy, Stoicism, or Roman household codes (Balch 1984, Martin 1986). And the seeds of such thinking produced the fruit of the story of Paul, Onesimus, and Philemon.

First Peter also sets conditions on the household codes. In a setting of crisis, submission to human authority is for the Lord's sake. Christians were suffering "unjustly" at the hands of tyrannical masters (2:19-20), husbands (3:6), and local government officials (2:14, 3:14, 17). The purpose of the code in 1 Peter is not to insist on conformity to traditional values, but pragmatically to steer a prudent line. The appeal is for Christian commitment even when it involves suffering (Martin 1986).

There was no question of inferior nature accepted here for all are called to live as "servants of God" (2:16). Christ as the "Suffering Servant of God" is the model to follow (2:21-24). In the address to slaves, the terms used elsewhere in the codes for *servant (doulos)* and *master (kurios)* are not used here. Rather, the terms *household servants (oiketai)* and *despots (despotai)* are used. The reason for such a change is that the author has already used the term *servant* to refer to every Christian (2:16) and *master* (or *Lord*) for God (2:15).

Roman rulers might not judge "justly" as God has ordained that they should (2:13-14) and as he himself does (2:21-23), but are to be submitted to for the Lord's sake. Christian wives are to submit to pagan husbands for the purpose of evangelism (3:1-2) and are not to fear them (3:6). Christian husbands are called to a relationship with their wives quite different from the cultural norm. In fact, a most revolutionary concept appears here: the husband's spiritual vitality is dependent upon the way he treats his wife.

The most significant critique of the husband-wife pair of the household code in 1 Peter would be immediately obvious to the original hearers of that epistle. And yet, without historical and cultural background, readers today would all but miss it. The Christian women addressed in 1 Peter 3 were married to pagan husbands. And yet, despite the norms of the Roman (and, in fact Jewish) culture of that time, these women were allowed the freedom of religious choice. The typical Roman concern is expressed by Plutarch:

> It is becoming for a wife to worship and know only the gods that her husband believes in, and to shut the door tight upon all queer rituals and outlandish superstitions. For with no god do stealthy and secret rites performed by a woman find favor (Plutarch 1928).

Even while addressing women in this text by appealing to the social code of the day, this text in 1 Peter assumes their religious independence from their pagan husbands (cf. 1:18, 4:3, 4). These women were encouraged to keep their faith and not to fear their husbands who likely had been expressing extreme displeasure and concern at their wives conversions. So, when those women heard this epistle in a service of worship they heard a proclamation of freedom, religious responsibility, and increased value. Had their pagan husbands heard that same text, they would have heard insubordination and anarchy. And how would they have heard the words to their wives, "Do not give way to fear"? But, oh, how differently this text is read today.

Many scholars have recognized the difference in the way the household codes are used in 1 Timothy and Titus. The predominant attitudes of the culture of that day seem to have been adopted in the church by this time (Jewett 1975). In these texts, there is no instruction to the dominant members of the pairs that is comparable to the leveling effect of the Colossians or Ephesians texts. And yet, the motivation for the concern that women and slaves ought to be subject is stated in Titus as the desire for the church to win the acceptance of society. This is still not the Roman appeal to an inborn nature of superior or inferior. It is a pragmatic appeal not unlike the exhortation to prayer in 1 Timothy 2:1-3. The purpose for both instructions is "that we may live peaceful and quiet lives" which will provide the opportunity for salvation of all.

The passage in 1 Timothy most often quoted in the debate about women in ministry is part of a loose expression of the old household codes (2:11-15). And yet, even here in the most conservative expression of the code in the New Testament, the reason for submission is not the nature of the creation, but rather the story of the Fall. This appeal to woman's greater culpability in the Fall cannot be taken as a theological absolute. The Genesis account (Genesis 3) here referred to, does not assign such a meaning to the woman's succumbing first to temptation. And the Apostle Paul when referring to the Fall, talks about Adam's sin (Romans 5:12-14). In fact the claim made in 1 Timothy 2:14, that "Adam was not the one deceived; it was the woman who was deceived and became a sinner" cannot be equated with the Genesis or Romans references to this event. It is much more like the rabbinical speculations of that time as expressed, for example by Philo, the Apostle Paul's older contemporary:

> . . . the woman, being imperfect and deprived by nature, made the beginning of sinning; but man, as being the more excellent and perfect nature, was the first to set the example of blushing and being ashamed, and indeed of every good feeling and action (Balch 1981, 84).

Long ago, Adolph von Harnack presented his theory to explain the changes in social attitudes from Jesus' followers and the earliest expression of the church to Christianity as represented by the pastoral epistles (1 Timothy and Titus). He observed the following progression: (1) the radical perspectives of Jesus, (2) unconventional freedom for women in the earliest congregations, (3) conditional appeals to the cultural norms by use of the household codes and (4)

27

uncritical acceptance of Graeco-Roman values. He called this progression a Hellenization (being made Greek) process (Balch 1984).

While Harnack's theory is too simplistic, his observation of a gradual Hellenization has merit. This is best observed when Jewish traditions about slavery are observed. The Jews were never to forget that they were once slaves. In fact, the central story of the Torah (first five books of the Old Testament) is the Exodus. God freed the Hebrew slaves from their Egyptian lords. Therefore, slavery was conditioned with many protections in Israel. Slaves were to be freed after six years of service and moreover, were to be sent off with blessings and liberal provisions for livelihood (Exodus 21:1-6, Deuteronomy 15:12-18). Therefore, slavery was not to become a perpetual institution. There was no elitism involved. This was quite a different expression from Aristotle's concept of a natural hierarchy.

Careful study of the household codes reveals a very different usage in the New Testament than is claimed in some popular teaching of today. While the codes expressed a "reversion to convention" (Pagels 1974), the motivation in the New Testament was for pragmatic concerns and was not based upon some concept of natural order by creation. The popular interpretation of these codes today is more Aristotelian than Christian and ignores the impact of the spiritual qualifications placed upon them by the New Testament writers.

Argument from Creation Accounts

In the above examination, the arguments from the creation accounts have been referred to briefly. A more detailed study is required for our purposes. The creation account of Genesis 1 presents a creation in which male and female are together created in the image of God (cf. 5:1-2). The second creation account that Paul appealed to includes two aspects that have been used to promote a hierarchical model. First, woman is created after man, and is taken from his rib. While it might be said that the Apostle Paul's words in 1 Corinthians 11 argue an order of priority in the basis of this text, the original text does little to support the development of a model of dominance/subordination. The "rib" is the symbol of correspondence between man and woman. The man and the woman belong to each other in a qualitatively different way than they belong to the animals: "The unique closeness of her relationship to the man is underlined above all through the fact that she is created, not from the earth but out of the rib from man himself" (Wolff 1974, 94). If anything, the woman is distinguished from the animals who are not suitable for relationship with the man, who are subordinate to him. The woman's superiority for relationship with the man (over the animals), not her inferiority in relationship to the man is the point of the story.

The second aspect of the text used to support the dominance of man is that woman was created to be a "helper" for man (Gen. 2:20). Yet, this term *helper* is the same term used of God in his relationship with man (e.g. Exod. 18:4, Isa. 30:5, Ps. 146:5). There is no connotation of subordination in the term, only that of correspondence. The term has been misapplied when it is interpreted to mean that woman was created to be servile to man.

The concept of subordination is first referred to in Genesis 3:16 as a consequence of the Fall. Speculation on that text is a late development in Judaism, occurring first in the second century B.C. (Balch 1986, 97). "The Old Testament [itself] does not emphasize the subordination of wives" (Balch 1986, 97). If the consequence of the Fall is the subordination of women, should that subordination be lifted up as the ideal? It seems obvious that it is rather a part of the fallen creation, the old order, which in the Apostle Paul's mind is passing away.

Clearly Jewish culture was patriarchal, especially in Jesus' day. Yet, women were generally accorded more value in the Jewish culture than in the Roman world. It is certain that misogynism (extreme devaluation of women) was a late rabbinical development that was later adopted by some of the church fathers of the second and third centuries. Such attitudes cannot be based upon the creation accounts of Scripture.

The Eschatological Age of the Spirit

Another line of reasoning in the discussion of women in ministry makes reference to Joel's prophesy as quoted by Peter on the day of Pentecost (Acts 2). The implications of this prophesy are developed by the Apostle Paul in his teaching of the new creation, the new Adam (Romans 5), and a New Israel—all eschatological (end times) categories. (Dr. Marie Strong in chapter 1 reviews this material in more detail.)

In the line of such thinking, the Apostle Paul develops the idea of the new time in which "we are no longer under the law." It is the time now in which "faith has come" (Gal. 3:25). In this discussion, Paul speaks of the inception of that faith and baptism into Christ. In Christ (here in the corporate sense of the church): "There is neither Jew nor Greek, slave nor free, male nor female, for you are all one in Christ Jesus" (Gal. 3:28).

The threefold distinctions excluded here correspond to popular formulas that maintained such distinctions. The morning prayer of the Jewish male includes the thanksgiving that he was not created a Gentile, a slave, or a woman (Stern 1928). Against the Roman expression of distinction and division in the household codes and Jewish man's prayer the Apostle Paul proclaims the positive dissolution of all such realities. The fact that it is more than a visionary and "spiritual" ideal is proved by the fact that precisely the human structures of these distinctions were addressed in the life and practice of the early church. (For example, Peter's vision of Acts 10 is lived out in Caesarea and then was the motivation for inclusion of the Gentiles in Acts 11.) The unity for which Paul appeals is to be a reality (Eph. 2). Not only does Paul insist upon living out such a vision, but he also attempts to do just that himself. (He insists upon the same thing as a norm in the church in his confrontation with Peter.) He also appeals to Philemon for the sake of Onesimus on the basis of such convictions. His practice in ministry with Christian women was the culminating expression of his conviction that "in Christ, all things are made new" (2 Cor.

5:17). Nevertheless, "whereas Paul's ban on discrimination on racial or social grounds has been widely accepted *au peid de la lettre* (sic.), there has been a tendency to restrict the degree to which there is no "male and female" (Bruce 1982, 189). In Galatians, the context may be limited to a discussion of baptism, which is open to all (as opposed to circumcision, which was the old sign of the law). "But the denial of discrimination which is sacramentally affirmed in baptism holds good for the new existence 'in Christ' in its entirety" (Bruce 1982, 190). F.F. Bruce's conclusion seems to be the best given both content and context:

> No more restriction is implied in Paul's equalizing of the status of male and female in Christ than in his equalizing status of Jew and Gentile, of slave and free person. If in ordinary life existence in Christ is manifested openly in church fellowship then if a Gentile may exercise spiritual leadership in church as freely as a Jew, or a slave as freely as a citizen, why not a woman as freely as a man? (Bruce 1982, 190).

Theological Synthesis

The evidence selected and analyzed above creates cumulative argument for the inclusion of women, not only in the life of the church but also, in the function of ministry of the church. The visionary expression of Jesus' life and ministry with women infers it. The practice and expressions of mutuality of the Apostle Paul indicate the same. The household codes are best thought of as cultural expressions appealed to for pragmatic concerns and in their very qualification indicate an open future. The appeals to "creation order" are not so conclusive as those such as Bill Gothard would like us to believe and at any rate will not support the exclusion of women in ministry. Finally, the idealism of the eschatological age, the age of the Spirit, was certainly understood to have come into being at Pentecost. The implications were gradually recognized and affirmed in the life and practice of the church. The record of the New Testament is the story of that process.

The question of degrees of implementation, which the evidence implies, has been argued by some along the lines of function versus office. This thinking reasons that women may function in ministry but are not to be allowed to the formal legitimization of offices. A derivation of this idea is that women be allowed legitimization in an office only where they would not be "over men." In this case, a woman always functions under the authority (and so supervision) of a man. Such a distinction seems artificial, especially given the history of differentiation between clergy and laity. Even the Catholic Biblical Association's committee on the Role of Women in Early Christianity makes the following observation:

> In the primitive Church . . . ministries were complex and in flux, and the different services later incorporated into the priestly ministry were performed by various members of the community. . . . Thus, while Paul could speak of charisms as varying in importance . . . the New Testament evidence does not indicate that one group controlled or exercised all ministries in the earliest Church. Rather the responsibility for ministry, or service, was shared. . . . The Christian priesthood as we know it began to be established no earlier than the end of the first or the beginning of the second century.

Therefore, the committee recognized that all of the members of the body were understood to have been gifted for upbuilding ministries (Eph. 4:12; cf. vv. 15-16, 1 Cor. 12:7, 12-31, Rom 12:4-5). Women did perform ministry and exercise functions that were later defined by offices of ministry. Therefore, the committee concluded, against their own church traditions, that "the New Testament evidence, while not decisive by itself, points toward the admission of women to priestly ministry" (Catholic Biblical Quarterly 1979). It has already been noted that nowhere does the New Testament speak explicitly of women in church office. Only three discussions in the New Testament even touch on the participation of women in worship services. The basic concern of these texts is for proper conduct. First Corinthians 14 cannot mean that women are not to pray and prophesy (preach) in public assembly (cf. 1 Cor. 11:3-6). Likewise, the prohibition in 1 Timothy 2:11-15 runs counter to the evidence of their texts in the Scripture.

The household codes cannot be appealed to for the general supervision of all women functioning in ministry in the Church. In their contexts they are applied to husbands and wives only and are discussions of proper interpersonal relations in the family (and perhaps to that particular family in their experience in worship). A further point is that if the Apostle Paul were applying the household codes to ministerial function in the Church, he never would have mentioned Priscilla's name first in the lists. He was already breaking tradition to mention her name at all and more, to list her as a teacher of Apollos.

While early freedoms for women in the New Testament were later restricted along society conventions, the same impetus for change regarding the status of women existed in the Church as for Gentiles and slaves. The participation of women in services of worship and the inclusion of them in ministry are evidence of that. The earlier motivation for accepting societal role or status, the idea that Jesus was returning immediately (1 Corinthians) was soon replaced by the need for the tolerance of society and harmony in mixed-religion homes. Despite all of this, the Church has never lost the vision of itself as being an expression of the Kingdom of God come. The early Church of God simply saw itself as being faithful to the new realities called into being "in Christ" when they recognized women in the function and offices of leadership in the Church. The best understanding of Scripture calls for us to be so visionary today.

Susie Stanley

Susie Stanley is an ordained minister in the Church of God. She is currently Professor of Church History and Women's Studies at Western Evangelical Seminary, Portland, Oregon. Her Ph. D. degree in American Religion and Culture was conferred by Iliff School of Theology/University of Denver, Colorado. She has received the Louise Hunderup Award (1986) for contribution and service in Ecumenical Ministries in Oregon in the area of religious education.

She has written extensively for Dictionary of Christianity in America and has contributed articles to Colloquium, Vital Christianity, Church of God Missions, and Christian Leadership.

Susie is guest lecturer and speaker in workshops and seminars for many Christian Fellowships. Her teaching ministry has included many guest presentations in Oregon, California, Michigan, and Colorado.

Chapter 3:

Women Evangelists in the Church of God at the Beginning of the Twentieth Century

Susie Stanley

From its inception, the Church of God affirmed women's participation in ministry. It is crucial to be aware of our foremothers. We are blessed with so many of them! They form a cloud of witnesses who can inspire us as we "run with perseverance the race marked out for us" (Hebrews 12:1).

Women in the Church of God today follow in the footsteps of the pioneers who blazed a trail that has become overgrown with weeds. Some people have forgotten that there ever was a trail. A diminishing number of runners has been able to keep the way barely visible. The path needs to be worn down by women who answer the call to follow the path made by women preachers as they engaged in the task of spreading the gospel.

An analysis of early issues of the *Gospel Trumpet* reveals the significant involvement of Church of God women in evangelistic outreach. The "News from the Field" column in the *Gospel Trumpet* records information for eighty-eight women active in ministry during the years 1891 and 1892. This chapter will document the place of the Church of God in the Wesleyan/Holiness Movement and the implications of holiness doctrine for the acceptance of women preachers. Then the chapter will highlight four early women evangelists in the Church of God: Mother Sarah Smith, Mary Cole, Nora Siens Hunter, and Lena Shoffner Matthesen.

Wesleyan/Holiness Affirmation of Women in Ministry

The Church of God endorsed and encouraged women to preach during the late nineteenth century when very few denominations ordained women. Why was the Church of God so supportive of women preachers during its early years? The answer lies in its roots within the Holiness Movement. The Holiness Movement's affirmation of women preachers has been documented by Nancy Hardesty and the Daytons (Hardesty 1984; Ruther 1979, 225-254). Sociologist Bryan Wilson notes the positive correlation between holiness doctrine and women's public involvement in religious activities:

> The Holiness Movement in its varied forms brought women to the fore, perhaps more than any previous development in Christianity. This was not through the leadership of any one woman, but was a widely diffused tendency. . . . It was the first development in Christianity which admitted them to positions of influence on any wide scale, both because external

influences sanctioned and, because the freedom emphasized in the new movement ignored traditional Christian precepts on the subjects (Wilson 1970).

The Church of God emerged out of the broader Wesleyan/Holiness Movement late in the nineteenth century. This movement, drawing on the theology of John Wesley, promoted the doctrine of holiness or sanctification, which is understood as a second distinct work of grace following the experience of conversion, the first work of grace. At conversion, a person's sins are forgiven, while sanctification destroys the sinful nature of the individual, resulting in purity of heart. Other churches that resulted from the Holiness Movement include the Wesleyan Church, the Free Methodist Church and the Church of the Nazarene.

Phoebe Palmer, a Methodist laywoman, popularized Wesleyan/Holiness doctrine in the United States (White 1986 and Raser 1987). Her preaching and writing ministry extended from the late 1830s until her death in 1874. She based her doctrine of holiness on Wesley's writings but adapted it to the revivalistic atmosphere of her day. Palmer insisted that a sanctified person must testify publicly to the experience of holiness or it could be lost. As a result of this requirement, many women spoke in public for the first time. Since the distance from testifying to preaching is a short one, many women in the Wesleyan/Holiness Movement became evangelists.

The understanding of the source of ministerial authority in the Holiness Movement also resulted in the acceptance of women as preachers. The Holiness Movement affirmed women in leadership positions because of its emphasis on the Holy Spirit. It ascribed authority to the Holy Spirit rather than locating authority in the priestly office, where authority is transmitted by ecclesiastical leadership. Women generally hold prominent positions in groups who derive authority from the Holy Spirit. The Spirit is no respecter of persons but dispenses gifts of ministry to both men and women. F.G. Smith, an early leader in the Church of God, articulated this prophetic view of authority in a letter to a "sister in Christ":

Again, I call your attention to the organization of the church by the Holy Spirit. A man is an evangelist because he has the gift of evangelizing. It is not because he is a man, but because he has that particular gift. The gift itself is the proof of his calling. If a woman has divine gifts fitting her for a particular work in the church, that is the proof, and the only proof needed, that that is her place. Any other basis of qualification than divine gifts is superficial and arbitrary and ignores the divine plan of organization and government in the church (Smith 1920, 2).

Other Church of God authors also emphasized that the Holy Spirit dispenses gifts equally upon women and men. For instance see Sarah Bishop, "Should Women Preach?" (*Gospel Trumpet,* June 17, 1920, page 9,) and [George L. Cole], "The Labor of Women in the Gospel," (*Gospel Trumpet*, December 28, 1905, page 1).

Holiness believers patterned themselves after the early or primitive church which also emphasized the work of the Holy Spirit. Holiness adherents documented the role of women in primitive Christianity and sought to restore to women the place they had initially filled in the church. Luther Lee, a founder of the Wesleyan Church, argued: "All antiquity agrees that there were female officers and teachers in the Primitive Church" (Lee 1975).

Grounded firmly in the Wesleyan/Holiness tradition, the Church of God affirmed women in ministry because it stressed the authority of the Holy Spirit who gifts both men and women to serve in all capacities of religious work. By so doing, leaders believed they were modeling themselves after the early church.

Empowerment Equips Women for Ministry

Empowerment accompanies the experience of sanctification. Holiness leaders such as Phoebe Palmer traced the doctrine to Pentecost where the first Christians received God's power. Jesus had instructed his followers to stay in Jerusalem "until you are clothed with power from on high"

(Luke 24:49). Palmer proclaimed: "Holiness is power" (Palmer 1859, 206). Wesleyan/Holiness women attributed the power that accompanied sanctification to the Holy Spirit. It was this power that enabled women to overcome any hesitation about preaching and that sustained them when their right to preach was questioned. Equipped with the empowerment of the Holy Spirit, women challenged the custom that said it was unwomanly to speak in public.

Empowerment by the Holy Spirit often resulted in a dramatic personality change. Women lost their timidity when they were sanctified (Loveland 1977; Stanley 1987; Wickersham 1900). Holy Spirit power transformed timidity into "holy boldness."

Empowerment also enabled women to overcome the "man-fearing spirit" that initially had caused them to restrict their religious activities. Women consistently reported that prior to sanctification they had allowed the fear of male censure to stifle them. Mother Sarah Smith described her experience of sanctification: "I was filled with power and the Holy Ghost and such boldness. All that man-fearing spirit was taken away, and my heart was overflowing with perfect love that was so unspeakable and full of glory" (Smith 1902). The power which accompanied the experience of sanctification enabled women to crush the paralyzing "man-fearing spirit."

The Biblical Basis for Women in Ministry

I Sanctification being filled with power of H.S — the same —

The interpretation of the Bible by Holiness leaders endorsed women's right to preach (Stanley 1987, 304-329). Phoebe Palmer and B.T. Roberts wrote books providing a biblical support for women clergy. Alma White and William Godbey are among those who authored pamphlets on the topic (Palmer 1859; Roberts 1891; White 1921; Godbey 1891) Church of God interpretations of scriptures relating to women in ministry paralleled these holiness defenses (see Bishop 8-9; C.E. Brown 1939).

Grounded in the experience of Pentecost, the Holiness hermeneutic supporting women clergy also focused on Galatians 3:28, Psalm 68:11, and incorporated the accounts of prominent women in the Bible who provided models for women preachers.

At Pentecost, the divine commission was addressed to both sexes. This incident in the life of the early church documents women's ministry. Pentecost served as the precedent for women's leadership in the church. Mary Cole, who incorporated a brief defense of women preachers in her autobiography, pointed out that Acts 1:14 documented the presence of women, including Jesus' mother, at Pentecost. Acts 2:4 recorded that they all spoke as the Spirit gave them utterance. Cole asked, "Does not the 'all' include the women present? Was not their speaking as the Spirit gave utterance the act of a minister in preaching?" (Cole 1914). To Mary, the answer to both questions clearly was "yes."

B.T. Roberts, a founder of the Free Methodist Church, urged that Scripture used to oppose women preachers should be measured against the standard of Galatians 3:28: "Make this the *key text* upon this subject, and give to other passages such a construction as will make them agree with it, and all is harmony" (Roberts 1986, 55 and Mickelsen 1986, 179-186). F.G. Smith's view corresponded with that of Roberts. He referred to Galatians 3:28 as an "expression of basic principles" that "boldly declared a different standard for the kingdom of God" (Smith, 1920, 1; Bishop 1939; Brown 1939).

Many holiness leaders pointed out the mistranslation of Psalm 68:11 and quoted with favor Adam Clarke's translation of this verse, "of the female preachers there was a great host" (Clarke 3:342). Holiness writers claimed that the prophecy declared by this verse was being fulfilled by women in the Holiness Movement. Nora Hunter frequently quoted Psalm 68:11.

Supporters of women clergy in the Holiness Movement studied the Bible to discover women there who had served God in capacities of leadership. An article in the *Gospel Trumpet* listed Huldah, Deborah, Miriam and Anna (Bishop 1939, 8). The ministry of Jesus likewise corroborated the cause. Alma White often mentioned the woman of Samaria in her sermons because she illustrated God's approval of women's ministry (White 1935-1943). The events surrounding Jesus' death and resurrection provided evidence for holiness arguments favoring women in ministry. The popular refrain, "last at the cross, and earliest at the grave" was often invoked to comment on the loyalty of Jesus' women followers whom he entrusted with the message of his resurrection.

Holiness interpreters pointed out the ministry of women in the book of Acts and women who were co-workers with Paul. Mary Cole drew attention to Phoebe whom Paul commended in Romans 16:1. Rather than challenging the mistranslation of *diakonos* as servant, Cole took another approach. In response to those who argued that this verse restricted women's role in the church to domestic work, Cole argued:

> If the inference of this scripture is that a woman can serve the church by doing temporal work only, the preachers are not doing their duty, because in the second verse the Lord commanded the other ministers to assist Phoebe. If then the women's only service be to cook for the ministers, the minister, if they would obey this scripture, should certainly help the women cook (Cole 1914, 87).

Several factors contributed to the acceptance of women in ministry in the Holiness Movement: the requirement that all persons publicly testify of their experience of sanctification, the emphasis on the Holy Spirit and the Holiness hermeneutic. Like other prophetic religious groups, the Holiness Movement encouraged women to defy the traditional stereotype that precluded women's leadership in religious activities.

The affirmation of women clergy is a distinguishing characteristic of the Wesleyan/Holiness Movement. Holiness leaders quoted scripture passages to endorse women's expanded role in the church and criticized interpretations of verses that purportedly prohibited women's involvement in preaching and other leadership activities. The Holiness Movement encouraged women to preach by claiming that it was their Christian duty. Moving beyond rhetoric, holiness churches ordained women in unprecedented numbers thus facilitating and, at the same time, legitimizing women's fulfillment of their duty to God. (Unfortunately, many Holiness groups have experienced a significant decline in women preachers over the years. It is important to note, however, that of twenty-one denominations listed in a recent study, the majority of women clergy come from holiness or pentecostal churches; women in the other Protestant denominations combined make up a minority of all women clergy.

In 1986, holiness and pentecostal groups in the study reported 8,558 women clergy, while fourteen other denominations listed 8,117 women clergy. The Assemblies of God (3,718) and the Salvation Army (3,220) account for the bulk of the former figure. Examining statistical trends over the last ten years, however, presents a bleaker picture. The three groups that showed a decline in women clergy since 1977 are the International Church of the Foursquare Gospel (-138), the Church of the Nazarene (-71) and the Wesleyan church (-129). The Church of God [Anderson, Indiana] reported the smallest gain (+3). For further analysis of Church of God statistics, consult Chapter 9 and appendices (Eculink 1988). 1988).

The following section of this chapter will briefly summarize the lives and ministries of several prominent women evangelists in the early years of the Church of God.

Biographies of Women Evangelists

Mother Sarah Smith

Mother Sarah Sauer Smith shared biographical information in *Life Sketches* which she wrote in 1901 (published 1902). Born on September 20, 1822, in Summit County, Ohio, Sarah Sauer received only three months of formal education, first at a German school when she was twelve and later at an English school. She described her childhood briefly, "I was raised strictly moral" (Smith 1902, 3).

She described her conversion in 1842: "While the clock was striking nine, I sprang to my feet a new woman. Oh, how God did fill my soul with joy and glory and such sweet

peace that I walked the floor praising God!" (Smith 1902, 6).
Neither her parents nor her church shared Sarah's newfound
joy. Her parents forbade her to go to prayer meetings or to
pray in secret. Sarah was further dismayed that the Lutheran
church of her birth refused to let her pray in the service. She
was eventually cast out of the Lutheran church.

Smith experienced sanctification in 1859 although it was
not until four years later that she first heard that term used
to describe the experience. She described the struggle that
ensued as she sought sanctification. "I could say yes to
everything until God said, 'Are you willing to work for me?'
Then the devil saw his last chance and said, "If you promise
to work for God you will have to leave home and your
husband will not let you go' " (Smith 1902, 16). Mother
Smith recalled that "the death struggle commenced." The
victory was hers. She reported that friends were astonished
at the change in her personality as a result of sanctification
that transformed her fearfulness into boldness.

In Jerry City, Ohio, Sarah Smith led a group of thirty-five
people who met four times a week in a holinesss association.
Smith first encountered Daniel Sydney Warner, a prominent
leader during the early days of the Church of God, through
his writings. Someone sent her one of his first papers, which
included an article on the one Church. Smith agreed with
Warner's position: "I would not dare to say a word against
it, for that was just what I was looking for" (Smith 1902,
23). Warner and a colleague, Alexander J. Kilpatrick, visited
the group in 1882. As a result, twenty people stood to
declare their freedom from sectarianism, including Sarah
Smith who asked that her name be removed from both the
Methodist Episcopal class book and from a United Brethren
holiness band book (Smith 1892). Smith frequently wrote to
the *Gospel Trumpet*, Warner's periodical, detailing her evangelistic work in Ohio (Allison 1974).

After declaring her freedom from all denominational affil-
iations, Smith wrestled with another decision.

> The Lord began to show me that I must break up
> housekeeping and go into the gospel work. . . . I said

> I was too old, as my age was 61, and I have no
> education but the Lord told me what to do. I said
> who will take care of my husband? He said the
> children and He would care for him. . . . That eve-
> ning I went home and told my folks what I would
> do, and in ten days I was on my way, cut loose from
> house and home, not knowing whether I would even
> see my home again (Smith 1902, 28, 30).

Smith shared her decision with her husband at the breakfast table by informing him, "I am done cooking for farming." Mr. Smith finished eating his breakfast, walked out,
and then returned, asking how soon she would have to
leave. When his wife replied she would leave in ten days or
two weeks, he responded with, "I will get you some money"
(Smith 1902, 33). One wonders what else transpired between
the two. One brief paragraph in her account covers the con-
versation. We can imagine the reaction today if a sixty-one
year-old woman suddenly announced she had been called to
evangelistic work that would require her to leave family and
home and travel across the country.

Mother Smith headed for Beaver Dam, Indiana where she
met D.S. Warner, Barney Warren, Frances (Frankie) Miller,
and Nannie Kigar. The five of them composed the first
evangelistic company of the Church of God. Smith sang
high tenor in the quartet. Her responsibilities also included
testifying, praying, and occasional preaching. She was known
for her glowing testimonies during which she sometimes
shouted, clapped, and even jumped (*Quest*, 72). The company formed in 1885 and worked together for over four
years, holding meetings in ten states and Canada. In each
location, whether a church or a brush arbor, they "preached
the whole truth—justification, sanctification, one church,
and divine healing" (Smith 1900, 312).

Looking back, Mother Smith recalled that God protected
the company from mobs in several cities. At Grover, Indiana,
the group was showered with eggs but no one was hit. The
company never took up a collection during all their travels,
but relied on God to supply their needs. Mother Smith
reported that the members of the company worked well

together: "We were all of one heart and one mind and saw eye to eye" (Smith 1902, 34). Warner's company provided a model for others. The "flying ministry" offered the opportunity for many women to serve as evangelists (*Quest*, 73).

How did a woman of Smith's age endure traveling by lumber wagon and other conveyances of the late 1800s? No complaints appear in her sketches. Mother Smith's strength, both physical and spiritual, must have been phenomenal.

Mother Smith's spirit and enthusiasm inspired others. Mary Cole recalled, "Mother Sarah Smith, who sat right in front of the pulpit and who always encouraged the ministers and held up their hands with her 'Amen! Praise the Lord'" (Cole 1914, 189). Mary Cole also wrote of Mother Smith's personal support, "Mother Smith was quite helpful, as the enemy tried to depress and crush" (Cole 1914, 147).

Mother Smith's obituary in the *Gospel Trumpet* summarized her ministry:

> She has for many years been a faithful mother in Israel. Wherever she was known, she was known as "Mother Smith." She was known not only by that name, but she was known to be a firebrand for God and a terror to Satan. For more than 20 years she has attended various camp meetings of the saints, and during this time she was widely known. . . . Her testimonies were generally so inspiring as to set the camp meeting blazing as it were, with the praises and manifestations of the glory of God. . . . While she has gone to her reward above, the church on earth has lost a staunch advocate of the full gospel in this evening of time (*GT* 1908, 8).

Just as Deborah arose as a mother in Israel (Judges 5:7), Sarah Smith arose in the early days of the Church of God to inspire and encourage others to participate in the work of the Lord.

Mary Cole

Mary Cole was born on a farm near Decatur, Iowa, on August 23, 1853. She was the seventh of twelve children—

eight boys and four girls. When she was one year old, her family moved to Illinois. Two years later, they moved to Missouri where Mary spent the rest of her childhood and young adulthood. Health problems plagued her from the age of two when she began having spasms. By the age of fifteen, she was an invalid, spending five months at a time in bed.

At the age of seventeen Mary joined the Methodist Episcopal Church South, on probation, but her conversion did not occur until the next year on May 3, 1871. About four weeks after her conversion, she first heard about the doctrine of sanctification from her oldest brother, who was a minister. She sought and attained the experience the same day Jeremiah talked to her.

> When I received the sanctifying grace, I did not think of demonstration, or of great feeling, or of anything of that kind: I simply consecrated all a living sacrifice, and reckoned myself dead indeed unto sin and alive unto God through our Lord Jesus Christ. I met the conditions and believed that the work was done (Cole 1914, 14).

Cole's "conditions" matched Phoebe Palmer's theology of sanctification. Palmer, too, stressed that emotion did not necessarily accompany the experience of holiness. Palmer described sanctification as a two-part process, the person must consecrate or sacrifice his/her life through Christ and then have faith that the work was accomplished (Palmer 1859, 245). Mary mentioned reading Palmer's and John Wesley's books and also the books of Mrs. Fletcher and Hester Ann Rogers, British Methodist leaders of the eighteenth century.

At the age of twenty-two, Mary attended a camp meeting sponsored by several denominations. It was there that God said to her, "Go preach my gospel." Mary responded by making excuses: "Lord, I am not talented; my education is so meager; there is no one to go with me; and besides, I have a stammering tongue" (Cole 1914, 51). Mary returned home and reported God's will for her future to her Methodist Episcopal class leader. He responded by saying: "You are a pretty looking thing to be called to preach." Mary recorded that she agreed with his assessment but she did not know what to say so she replied: "I do not believe that every one called to preach will have to stand in the pulpit; a person may preach by his life and conduct" (Cole 1914, 52-53).

Mary remained single but she was engaged to be married at age twenty-six. She broke off the engagement when God made it clear to her that she should not marry. Mary did not even mention the young man's name. Again, we wonder about the unspoken. What pain did it cause Mary to break the engagement? Did she ever regret the decision? How did her fiance take the news?

Nearly seven years elapsed before Mary acted on her calling. In the interim, she was miraculously healed in the fall of 1880. God also cured her stammering to the extent that it did not interfere with her preaching. Mary received the gift of exhortation accompanied by the Spirit's power when she was healed. The first meeting she mentioned was in Wymore, Nebraska, with her brother George and Sister Lodema Kaser. She preached her first sermon at a holiness convention held in Salisbury, Missouri. The minister in charge of the service got up and announced that God had not given him a message. He further admonished that if the person who had the message did not deliver it, that person would be responsible to God. Although ministers and workers were sitting all around, Mary jumped to her feet immediately: "I had a message from heaven—burning words that went right into the hearts of the people. God made my tongue as the pen of a ready writer. The power of God was on me in such measure that I could hardly tell whether I was in heaven or on earth" (Cole 1914, 84). Mary often spoke of the divine power that made her preaching possible.

Mary reported that in her early evangelistic work there was considerable opposition to her preaching. At nearly every meeting, she had to explain the scriptural view on the matter of women preaching, responding to 1 Corinthians 14:35 and 1 Timothy 2:12, two texts that opponents claimed as proof that women should not preach. Mary would point out that they were misusing Scripture to support their false position.

For three years, Mary and her brother Jeremiah worked in Missouri, holding meetings in schoolhouses for two to four weeks' duration. Sometimes, they would separate and hold two meetings simultaneously in different locations. In such services, she would preach twice a day and three times on Sunday.

During her early ministry, Mary remained in the Methodist Episcopal Church which did not license women at that time. On first receiving the *Gospel Trumpet*, she burned it and wrote to Warner advising him she did not wish to receive any more copies. She was offended by the *Gospel Trumpet's* opposition to the licensing of preachers. Even though her own denomination refused to license her, Mary approved of ministerial licensing. Initially, she also opposed separatism. She believed that individuals who had experienced holiness and remained in their denominations would make their churches better. This was the position of many Methodists. D.S. Warner obviously forgave Mary for her early aversion to the movement since he wrote favorably of her is his diary, calling her "a chosen and anointed instrument of God to preach and testify to the Gospel of the grace of God" (Byers 1921).

Mary eventually left the Methodist Episcopal church by sending for her membership letter and then tearing it up. She did not share what made her change her mind, although she did tell about an experience that occurred the summer before at the quarterly conference of the denomination. She had been asked to conduct meetings in conjunction with the conference. During one of the services, the ministers met secretly and decided to stop her meetings. Mary was heartbroken: "I could not keep from crying. I had called the Methodist Church my mother; and now to think that my mother was treating me in this way, made me feel very bad" (Cole 1914, 124-125).

One rumor regarding Mary claimed she was one of the James Boys, the notorious outlaws, disguised as a woman. One wonders what the other rumors were!

Mary spoke of the helpfulness and encouragement women evangelists offered each other. Along with Mother Smith,

Sister Bolds was a great encouragement to Mary. Mary had an opportunity to encourage other women as well. Once, she felt led to visit a woman in Iowa who was "going through some deep trials." She described the problem this woman was having:

> Her difficulty seemed to be mainly self-accusation. In other words, she had set her spiritual standard so high that she could not live up to her own ideal. . . . Some of God's dear little ones who are very conscientious, sometimes look upon the Lord as a severe father. It seems to them that he, like Pharaoh, wants them to make brick without straw, to gather stubble. With this idea of God in mind, they have a hard time and fail to see him as a good, kind, loving heavenly Father, one whose heart is overflowing with mercy and compassion for his dear tired children, ready to make a way for their escape (Cole 1914, 272).

On another occasion, Mary visited Sioux Falls, South Dakota, to spend time with a sister "who was needing some special encouragement" (Cole 1914, 272).

Mary spoke of troubles during her services. Once, someone put red pepper on the stove located in the center of the room. Fumes from the pepper almost stifled the congregation. Twice during the same series of meetings, eggs were thrown at the workers but none found their mark. At a camp meeting in Mole Hill, West Virginia, a mob appeared, threatening to tear the tent down. Shots were exchanged between the mob and those who were defending the worshipers. Mary admitted that as several bullets whizzed near her, she ducked behind the canvas for protection. Afterwards, she laughed at herself for seeking such a flimsy refuge.

Preachers at camp meetings had an unusual method of determining who would bring the message. The first person to reach the pulpit at the appointed time was the one who preached. During one service at a camp meeting in Michigan, God made it clear to Mary that she should deliver the evening message:

I submitted the matter to the Lord, telling him that if he still wanted me to deliver the message, to hold the brother back until it would not appear that I was trying to get ahead of him. God wonderfully owned and blessed his Word, and a number of backsliders were reclaimed. After the service, the brother who had thought he had the message came to me and said, "Sister Cole, I did think I had the message, but the Lord blessed you." "Yes," I said, "the Lord blessed me in obeying but it took more grace than usual" (Cole 1914, 190).

It not only took an extra measure of grace, but the speed of an Olympic sprinter!

Mary conducted services primarily in Missouri and Kansas. She also mentioned holding camp meetings in Nebraska, Oklahoma, Indiana, Illinois, West Virginia, and Michigan. The greater part of her work in later years was with her younger brother, George, who first joined her in 1890. They conducted services in twelve states (Cole 1900, 349). Lodema Kaser also accompanied Mary over a period of seven years (Byers, Feb. 19, 1920). Kaser joined Mary and George later in Chicago and assisted in the mission work there for four years (Byers, Apr. 22, 1920, 5-6).

Mary and a company of six others traveled to California in 1894, holding services in Los Angeles, San Francisco, and Fresno. In Los Angeles, most of the company was under arrest for about three hours for preaching on the street. Mary did not mention if she were one of those arrested. After working in California for sixteen months, the company headed back east, stopping in Arizona for meetings in Phoenix.

Mary and her brother George settled in Chicago in 1898. They assisted there for one year before assuming responsibility for the rescue mission. The mission offered overnight lodging for five cents which included a free breakfast (Wickersham, 1900, 351). During her first winter in Chicago, Mary helped with meetings for homeless men in the slum district and conducted cottage meetings in private homes. In March 1903, workers began building a home and chapel which was finished by Christmas. This facility became the model for other missionary homes (Smith 1980, 232). Mary spent ten years in Chicago before moving to Anderson to care for her mother in the old people's home there. Mary died in the Anderson Old People's Home on August 27, 1940.

Nora Siens Hunter

While the name of Nora Hunter is associated with the formation and early years of the Women of the Church of God, she began her ministry as an evangelist (Neal 1951).

Nora Siens was born on August 16, 1873, in Kansas. When her mother died nine years later, her father placed Nora and her brother in a Soldier's Orphanage where Nora remained for five years. She then lived near Galesburg, Kansas, with relatives for two years. It was at the Meeker schoolhouse in Galesburg where Dr. S.G. Bryant was preaching that Nora experienced conversion in 1892. Bryant himself had been converted through the ministry of the company including Mary Cole and Lodema Kaser (*Herald*). Nora joined the Bryants, traveling with them for one year in evangelist work, primarily assisting in the area of music and personal work. Then she worked with William Smith and his wife, S.J. Smith, for several months. During the summer of 1893, she and another woman had the oversight of the Children's Home, which was adjacent to the Gospel Trumpet Company publishing plant, then located in Grand Junction, Michigan.

Nora probably preached her first sermon that summer in Grand Junction. With the encouragement of D.S. Warner, Nora began preaching at the age of nineteen. Warner, who was in the audience at Grand Junction, asked Nora to join his company, at that time consisting of himself, his new wife the former Frankie Miller, and F.G. and Birdie Smith. Nora traveled with them for about a year.

Nora was involved in the innovative ministry incorporating the Floating Bethel, a gospel houseboat built on a flatboat by G.T. Clayton. Workers advertised meetings by putting notices in bottles and throwing them overboard into the Ohio River. The intention was to notify towns downstream of their impending arrival (Byers Mar. 4, 1920). Gospel workers visited towns located along the Ohio River, distributing literature, holding tent meetings, and visiting the sick.

In the fall of 1894, Nora worked with W.J. and L.E. Henry, conducting services in Indiana and Ohio for two years (*GT* 1894). After this period of ministry, she met Lena Shoffner and they decided to form a team of two.

Nora conducted a meeting with Lena in Federalsburg, Maryland in the fall of 1895. This meeting was beset by troubles. First, the tent blew down. The two then rented a Quaker church five miles away that turned out to be occupied by hornets who resented their guests. The hornets proceeded to sting the congregation, making it very difficult for both the listeners and the preachers to keep their minds on the sermon. In spite of all the difficulties, a thriving congregation resulted from Nora's and Lena's efforts.

Nora met Clarence Edgar Hunter at the Grand Junction camp meeting. After their marriage on November 3, 1896, the couple traveled together, holding services in various locations. They were leaders in the Missionary Home in Fort Wayne, Indiana. They held several pastorates in Kansas, Indiana, and Pennsylvania before moving to Los Angeles. Though both of them were preachers, most often the major responsibilities for pastoring fell to Nora. About 1923, she and her husband began prayer meetings and Sunday schools in private homes. A year and a half later, when the group formed a congregation, Nora became the pastor.

She cooperated with the East Los Angeles Health Center by assisting the homeless in locating housing and helping newcomers find jobs and food. During this time, she also served on a government censoring board that was responsible for assessing movies, the California Conference on Child Health and Protection, and she chaired the State Committee on Character Education (*Herald*, 143).

A five-month trip to Europe and the Middle East in 1929 led Nora to organize the Woman's Home and Foreign Missionary Society. Founded in 1932, the group later shortened its name to Women's Missionary Society; currently it is called Women of the Church of God. Nora served as president from 1932 to 1948, maintaining a busy schedule. One summer she reported attending nineteen camp meetings. She retired from active involvement in 1948 and died on January 27, 1951. Known as "the church's sweetheart," Nora Hunter left a legacy that continues to provide opportunities for women to reach out to the people in need around the world. Her vision of women in ministry was that the women of the Church of God were a great host needing to be mobilized for action.

Lena Shoffner

Lena Shoffner was born on February 26, 1868, near Nishnabotna, Atchinson County, Missouri. She described her upbringing briefly in a short account of her life: "I had a very pious training from my parents. They forbade my going to worldly amusements, such as theaters, balls, and card and wine parties. Neither would they allow me to read novels or continued stories of any kind" (Shoffner 1900, 336). As a young working woman, she succumbed to the influence of those around her and abandoned her parents' strict standards. She came under conviction, which resulted in conversion in February 1886. Not until four years later when she attended a meeting held by D.S. Warner and company did she experience sanctification.

Before this time, Lena felt that God had wanted her to preach but she did not understand what her specific role should be. Insight came in 1892: God wanted her to become an evangelist. She left her family in January, expecting to be gone ten days, but two years passed before she would see them again. Her schedule of meetings took her from Arkansas City, Kansas, to Grand Junction, Michigan, and east through Pennsylvania. On November 4, 1893, she embarked for England. She conducted services in Liverpool, London, and Birkenhead before returning to the States on August 31, 1895.

After attending a camp meeting in Pennsylvania, Lena joined Nora Hunter for an evangelistic tour of Maryland during the fall of 1895. One meeting on this tour has been discussed above in the section on Nora Hunter.

Lena is probably most well known for the sermon she preached to an integrated congregation at the 1897 state camp meeting held near Hartselle, Alabama. The group met the legal requirement for segregation of blacks and whites by placing a rope down the middle of the tent, with blacks sitting on one side and whites on the other. Taking as her text Ephesians 2:14 ("For he is our peace, who hath made both one, and hath broken down the middle wall of partition between us" KJV), Lena preached one-and-a-half hours on the evils of racial prejudice. Her sermon found its mark; someone took down the rope and both races prayed together at the altar (*Quest*, 165).

Lena traveled to Oklahoma with co-worker, Mabel Ashenfelter, in the spring of 1904 to conduct meetings in Oklahoma City. While preaching one evening, a member of Firebrand, a rival holiness group, proceeded to the platform and proclaimed to Lena: "I rebuke thee in the name of the Lord." The individual claimed Lena was preaching incorrect doctrine and insisted she leave the pulpit. John W.V. Smith recounted what happened next:

> She stopped her sermon long enough to place her hand on her hip, look the opposer in the eye and tell him that they had paid rent for the hall and furnished it and if he did not like what he was hearing he could rent a place and preach as he wished (*Quest,* 129).

Obviously, the intruder had met his match!

A new congregation resulted from this series of meetings in Oklahoma City. Lena's ministry took on a new dimension when she agreed to conclude her evangelistic work and serve as the first pastor of the congregation with Mabel as her associate. Lena held this pastorate for eight years (Hale n.d.).

Lena met Ed Matthesen during the revival at Oklahoma City in 1904. They were married later that year. They worked together throughout Oklahoma until her death on October 10, 1936.

Conclusion

The four women discussed above are representative of hundreds of women in the Church of God who devoted their lives to Christian service. These women form "a great cloud of witnesses" who provide inspiration as we "run with perseverance the race marked out for us" (Hebrews 12:1).

Alice J. Dise

Alice Dise is a licensed minister of the Church of God. Her ordination is pending. Currently she is Associate Minister of the Vernon Park Church of God in Chicago, Illinois, with Reverend Claude Wyatt as pastor.

Alice has a B.A. degree from Trinity College of Deerfield, Illinois; she continued Bible studies at Moody Bible Institute, Chicago, Illinois; and she has completed studies in childhood education at Chicago State University. She is a certified teacher with the Evangelical Teacher Training Association.

For forty years she has worked in the church school as teacher and administrator. She has served on the Illinois State Board of Christian Education, and she has served as workshop leader for the national Board of Christian Education of the Church of God, Anderson, Indiana. She also teaches for the Chicagoland Christian Women's Conferences.

She has written and edited Vacation Bible School curriculum for Urban Outreach in Chicago, and she has authored curriculum materials for Warner Press, Anderson, Indiana. Dise speaks frequently for women's groups and special observances. She serves as preacher in Church of God pulpits and in other denominations. She also serves with other ministers in taking religious services to nursing homes.

Chapter 4:

Black Women in Ministry in the Church of God

Alice Dise

This chapter is dedicated to the countless numbers of black women, both past and present, who have given of themselves in the work and service of the Church of God. There is no complete list of their names, their individual contributions, or their dreams for the church. The names and labors that are mentioned here are but a small representation of the works of a much larger body of women. This is a tribute to those who have been called to serve and who have done so with a great sense of commitment and commission, and often amidst unbearable constraints.

In the service of the Lord, the black woman has forged ahead, never digressing under fire, because of foe or fatigue. There are no areas of service from which she has shied away. She has been preacher, evangelist, teacher, administrator, doorkeeper, cook, and prayer warrior. Her gifts and talents have been used "for the perfecting of the saints, for the work of the ministry, for the edifying of the body of Christ" (Ephesians 4:12). She has been called, knowing who it was who called her; she has been committed to the task, however large or small; and she has been commissioned, knowing what had to be done and where.

Many have given as their reason for serving, simply "their calling," needing no special honors or accolades. For example, Polly Walker, an early church woman, said, "I never felt to be a pulpit preacher or pastor of a congregation. My calling is to console and to do house-to-house evangelism and to hold street meetings which I began to do in 1914, when I was filled with the Spirit" (Davis 1985, 36).

One of the first black leaders of the Church of God was *Jane Williams* who lived in South Carolina. Dr. James Earl Massey in his book *An Introduction to the Negro Churches in the Church of God Reformation Movement* notes that Jane Williams started a congregation in Charleston, South Carolina, about 1886. This congregation became the headquarters for the growth of the Church of God in the South as the work spread from South Carolina to Alabama, North Carolina, Georgia, and Florida. Much of the work among blacks had its beginning under her influential preaching (Massey 1959, 19). From 1888 to 1898, Jane Williams worked in Augusta, Georgia. Letters written to her by D.S. Warner indicate that they shared common burdens for evangelization of the unsaved. In one letter to D.S. Warner, Jane Williams asked that the Warner group join in prayer for a meeting house that she planned to build in Augusta, Georgia, (*GT* 1898, 5). It is believed that she had knowledge of holiness before hearing of the Church of God Reformation Movement and that she brought much information and Bible knowledge to her ministry.

In the "Commemorative Booklet of the National Association of the Church of God" Wilfred Jordan describes several of the early pioneers of the 1890s who served as pastors (Jordan 1981). Among these pioneers was *Mary Frambo* who was born in slavery. She was a member of the AME Church and active in a prayer band. The holiness teachings of John Wesley were a part of her spiritual training. Later she came in contact with the message of the Church of God and she was one of the founders of the Martin Street Church of God in Atlanta, Georgia. She was a prayer warrior and a preacher evangelizing everywhere she went. When the family moved to Chicago she worked in the store front church on Giles Avenue (Beverly 1988). She was faithful to her call.

Other early pioneers of the 1890s who made notable contributions to the church were *Lena Cooper*, who was the first Church of God pastor in Evanston, Illinois and *Christine James*, *Katie Alexander*, and *Elizabeth Peters*, who were all active in the Church of God in Chicago, Illinois.

The campgrounds at West Middlesex, Pennsylvania, are the realization of a dream credited to *Brother E.* and *Mother Priscilla Wimbish*. She shared the dream and worked to bring it to fruition. Her dedication and commitment to the campground outweighed her love for personal belongings. One time during a period of crisis, an unpaid mortgage on the campgrounds made foreclosure imminent. Brother Wimbish was willing to mortgage his home to give the trustees the loan that they needed. Sister Wimbish was willing to go further. She agreed to sell their home, donate a thousand dollars, and loan the church seven hundred dollars to be repaid over a period of five years. She later said, "I'm glad I did it. I have seen many people helped and many souls saved and made happy, which makes me rejoice to know that I was obedient to the voice of God, an instrument in His hands for the work of His kingdom" (Davis 1985, 14).

"The National Association is the organizational result for legal ownership of an area near West Middlesex, Pennsylvania, first secured for camp meeting purposes by a small group of Blacks living in Western Pennsylvania and Eastern Ohio," says *Katie Davis*, author and preacher, who wrote the book *Zion's Hill at West Middlesex*, preserving the story of the dream of the Wimbish ministry (Davis 1985, 47).

Emma Alberta Nelson Crosswhite, wife, mother of three, pastor, and evangelist became a legend in her own time. She was born in 1882 in South Charleston, Ohio, to Charles and Louisa Nelson. She was just eight-years old when she sought the counsel of her great-grandfather. She told him about an experience she had had while at prayer. He cautioned her to trust the experience but to keep it secret lest others scoff at her in unbelief. Then he told her that God would use her life in an outstanding way.

She married Joseph Crosswhite and was living in Washington Court House, Ohio, when tuberculosis was diagnosed. The pastor of the Church of God was called. George Lorton prayed for Emma's healing, and she was healed. Blessed with healing and with new insight into the Word of God, Emma and her husband covenanted to build a Church of God fellowship in Washington Court House where they lived, hoping to build a black congregation. During the tent meeting that they conducted, only white persons found salvation. With the forty white converts, the Crosswhites formed the first Church of God congregation in Washington Court House, Ohio. George Lorton the white minister who had prayed for her healing became the first pastor of the group. Soon thereafter George Lorton ordained Emma Crosswhite to the ministry and she became the pastor. The church grew under her ministry serving both black and white in an interracial fellowship. She pastored this church for forty-seven years. She related to all classes and races, and the citizens of Washington Court House referred to her respectfully as "city pastor" (Biographical sketch n.d.).

On the West Middlesex Campground the Crosswhite cottage was a center for prayer and counsel. Those who were blessed by her ministry at the West Middlesex Camp Meeting lovingly called her "Mother Crosswhite."

Marcus Morgan writes that Blacks "were attracted to the message of salvation from sin and the unity of all believers" (Morgan 1951). This emphasis on unity gave hope that the Church of God was a place devoid of racial segregation or discrimination. After 1917, blacks tended to evangelize blacks, and whites evangelized whites (Telfer 1972). However, there were many congregations that were interracial fellowships. Women of all races and ethnic backgrounds have worked for the good of the church.

In 1933, Ozie Garrett felt her call to the ministry. She was the seventeen-year-old daughter of Eugene and Ola (Brown) Garrett living in Columbus, Ohio, where her father was pastoring. Her role model was Emma Crosswhite, and twenty-five years later in 1958, Ozie would follow Emma Crosswhite as pastor of the Washington Court House, Ohio, congregation.

In 1947, she entered full-time ministry as an evangelist, and in 1950, she became the first home missionary sent from the National Board of Home Missions to the deep South in Louisiana and Alabama. In 1953, Ozie was called by the Columbus, Nebraska, congregation to be their pastor. This was an all-white congregation and Ozie was the only black person in town. Moreover she was the only woman pastor in the state. She served this church for two years, and then she returned to Ohio to pastor in Cleveland.

Ozie and her husband George Wattleton pastored in Ohio for years, then answered the call to Liberty Road Church in Houston, Texas. Following her husband's death in Houston, Texas, in 1970, Ozie returned to full-time ministry as an evangelist. Her fiery preaching and indomitable spirit have marked her ministry. In 1983, she became the pastor of the East Atlanta, Georgia, congregation (Wattleton 1988).

Ozie Garrett Wattleton has been a recognized leader and minister by both the black and white national Church of God organizations. She has acknowledged her call and commitment by being commissioned to serve as evangelist, pastor, and home missionary. She has also served as a member of national agency boards. Wattleton says of her ministry, "I have worked to break down racial barriers" (Wattleton 1988).

Ivory Virginia Smith was converted in an "Evening Light" meeting in South Carolina. Immediately she began to witness and share her testimony with others. Long before she felt called to the ministry, she had helped to establish churches in South Carolina. Through her work in the church she met and married Early Downer. While their children were small, she was not allowed to preach in the churches, but she exhorted in prayer and testimony.

During the Depression, Ivory heard of the hard financial times at the Gospel Trumpet Company. She gave her most precious possession, a five-dollar gold piece that she had earned working on a farm. She felt that it should go to God's work.

The Downer family moved to New York City, and Ivory kept herself busy starting churches in the area, visiting and praying for the sick, and working wherever she could to take the story of Christ to others. Hattie, Ivory's daughter has followed in her mother's footsteps as preacher and teacher assisting in the work of the congregations in New York City, serving the hopeless, the powerless, and the homeless (Downer 1973).

Nancy McClure Ford was converted at the age of twenty and felt a definite call to the ministry at the age of twenty-two. The call was a deep conviction to enter the ministry, but she protested, "They don't like women preachers and nobody would listen to me preach (Anderson 1980, 51). Finally after a period of illness, she submitted. In recalling her early ministry she said:

> It was very hard when I came along for women to get into the ministry. Especially if you had any training and if you had a gift that men recognized, then you got in trouble. If I had a large crowd to hear me, then the pastor would not let me preach any more for a long time (Anderson 1980, 52).

Nancy did not seek ordination because it was not important to her. She just kept on preaching. She was well versed in the doctrines of the Church of God and when her husband Edward A. Ford was being ordained, the committee called Nancy to participate in the interview. After asking a few questions the ordination committee chairperson said, "No need to ask Sister Ford these questions; she knows it all. Send her on out" (Anderson 1980, 52). She was ordained in the church in Charlotte, North Carolina.

Nancy was a teacher and had planned to teach for a while, but God convinced her that she should go to seminary. The ministers did not want her to go to seminary and preached against it. Nevertheless she entered Johnson C. Smith University and was the first black graduate and the first female graduate with a divinity degree.

Nancy Ford ministered as preacher and teacher for fifty-four years. She pastored the First Church of God in Raleigh, North Carolina, for thirty-three of those years.

Many black women have planted, pastored, and supported churches. The white work in Houston, Texas, was planted by *Annie Hall; about 1909; Beatrice Sapp* planted churches in Alabama serving both black and white congregations; *Melinda Lewis* started a Bible study group in her home after receiving some Gospel Trumpet literature and in time started the church in New Orleans; *Agnes Coleman* ministered thirty-four years traveling from north to south and east to west preaching and teaching in house prayer meetings, tent meetings, street meetings, and in churches.

Willie Taplin Barrow's parents came into the Church of God when she was two or three years old. Her father became a pastor at that time. Having had much religious training at home, Willie was ready to make her decision to become a Christian when she was eleven years old.

At the age of seventeen, she told her father, "I feel that I want to preach." When he asked her if that was really what she wanted to do, she affirmed that she felt that God was calling her to preach. She had studied the Bible and could quote scriptures by memory about the church, salvation, sanctification, healing and creation, but she wanted an education to prepare for her ministry (Anderson 1980, 34).

She attended Warner Pacific College where she majored in psychology and studied for the ministry. An internship was part of the ministerial education at Warner Pacific College. Willie worked in the housing projects among the black people. A Sunday school was started, and as the work developed, the first black Church of God in Portland, Oregon, was begun with the help of Otis Brown. Her ministry included counseling, teaching, preaching, and baptizing. Willie asked to be ordained, but was told that she had to complete her degree before ordination. She married Clyde Barrow a year before graduation and was not ordained (Anderson 1980, 35).

Willie and her husband moved to Chicago and began to work with S.P. Dunn in the Langley Avenue Church of God. She directed the Christian Education program, built the youth department, organized street meetings, established jail workers, and directed the choir. She was not concerned about ordination until she was working on national committees. Then she was told that she had to be ordained before she could preach or serve on these committees. She applied for ordination since she was doing the work of the ministry. She went before the State Ordination Committee, and after an eight-hour examination she was approved for ordination (Anderson 1980, 36).

She is the National Executive Director and Chief Executive Officer of Operation PUSH. She is also an associate pastor at the Vernon Park Church of God in Chicago where Reverend Claude S. Wyatt and Reverend Addie Wyatt pastored.

Ministry and the church have played an active role for social change in the black community. *Addie Wyatt* exemplifies this specific kind of ministry when she served as Vice-President of the Amalgamated Meat Packers Union. From this platform Addie Wyatt influenced the lives of people not only in the United States, but internationally. Since retirement her interdenominational work for social justice on behalf of all people has continued. *Juanita Lewis* is committed to social work as her ministry also. She specializes in home and family life education. Her writing and teaching in workshops and seminars are ministering across the church. She has also served in ministry through the National Council of Churches on national and international committees.

Reverend Sarah Taylor has brought together the women of the National Association in a Ministry Fellowship, meeting for the purpose of praying and strengthening each for the work of the Lord and sharing concern for the issues confronting women in ministry. This network of women meets annually in different cities in an attempt to meet the needs of women ministering in the urban centers of the United States.

Black women have served and are serving in missions in countries and cultures around the world. *Hester Greer*, one of the first black missionaries in the Church of God served in Cuba; *Wilhelmina Fraser* served in the Caribbean; *Mary Morgan* served with her husband in India; *Sheila Sawyer* served with her husband in Barbados; *Gwendolyn Massey* served in Jamaica; and in the 1980's there are women who serve in overseas missions—*Ruth Ann Lambe* in Bermuda, *Sylvia Roaché* in Panama, *Amanda Ricketts* in Brazil, and *Evelyn Wilson* in Kenya.

Christian Education has been a significant part of ministry among black women. *Pansy Melvina Major Brown* has been a pioneer in the field of Christian Education and has dedicated herself to developing the highest quality training possible. She was the co-founder of the In-Service Institute, a ministry of the National Association for the pastors and other church leaders who had not had the opportunity for extensive formal training. *Verda Beach* serves as Associate Minister of Christian Education at Emerald Avenue Church of God in Chicago; *Cheryl Sanders* serves as Associate Pastor for Leadership Development at Third Street Church of God in Washington, D.C.; and *Diana Swoope* serves as Associate Pastor in the Arlington Church of God in Akron, Ohio; *Theodosia Cumberbatch* is a minister and theologian, and a past dean of the West Indies Theological College in Trinidad, West Indies; and *Yvonne Babb* serves as minister-evangelist and Christian educator in Barbados, British West Indies (Dulin 1980).

The roll call goes on and on. So many black women have served the church and have given their gifts and talents in service for God and their community. These women have served from the pulpit to the kitchen with honor, dignity, and pride. The history of the Church of God has been indelibly imprinted with their person, their labors, and their bequeathals. Their stories serve as a challenge to all women to become whatever God calls them to be as they note and appreciate the role models that have gone before them. When the "Evening Light" gives way to the "Morning Light" her works will "praise her in the gates."

Nilah Meier-Youngman

Nilah Meier-Youngman is an ordained minister in the Church of God. She has served as Director of Hispanic Ministries with the national Board of Church Extension and Home Missions. Currently she is Associate Professor of Language at Anderson University. She is in a doctoral program at Austin Presbyterian Seminary, Austin, Texas, in Cross Cultural Missions with emphasis on Hispanos.

Nilah grew up in Argentina and Brazil of missionary parents. Her college studies and teaching have furthered her involvement with people of Spanish and Portuguese cultures. She holds a Masters degree from the University of North Carolina at Durham in Spanish Classics. She also has a Master of Divinity degree from Christian Theological Seminary in Indianapolis, Indiana.

As Director of Hispanic Ministries she recruited pastors for newly established Hispanic congregations. She organized training seminars for leaders and developed materials for evangelism and mission. She has been guest lecturer and speaker for numerous mission conferences and conventions.

Chapter 5:

Hispanic Women in Ministry in the Church of God

Nilah Meier-Youngman

All through the ages women have responded to Jesus' call to share the liberating gospel. Hispanic women have lacked affirmation in entering the ministry. Just as the society has been male dominated, so also in the church, men have held the key positions of leadership in South America and in the Hispanic Church in the United States of North America.

However, there have been outstanding pioneer women who are forging a future for other women to follow. I recall how amazed I was, a girl of twelve, when I heard the news that a woman minister was coming to Argentina from Germany. Her name was Mina Finkbeiner. It made a deep impression on me that this single woman preached, held revivals, taught, and did all the tasks of ministry that men did.

At the age of seventeen I experienced an even greater surprise when I discovered that my own mother had been ordained in 1929 when she completed her training at the Gospel Trumpet Training School in Anderson, Indiana. All those years she and father had worked as the first Church of God pioneer missionaries from the United States in Brazil and Argentina and this "secret" had never leaked out! Nobody had asked, I suspect, and mother, very aware of the male dominance in the church, had never shared this fascinating fact! Whether recognized or not, mother's zeal and passion for her Lord never diminished in forty-two years of service in South America. Side by side with my father, David Meier, my mother, Lillian Meier, evangelized, visited new colonies, cared for nineteen orphans, taught hundreds of children, organized youth and women's groups, prayed for the sick, and proclaimed the Savior everywhere she went.

Today, Tabita Meier Kurrle, Lillian's youngest daughter carries on the work of missions and ministry in the neighboring country of Paraguay. Tabita and her husband, Martin, direct a primary school and pastor three congregations.

Panama

The year 1988 marks seventy-five years for the Church of God (Iglesia de Dios) in Panama. Two women have played significant leadership roles in the life of the church there: Edith Peters and Daisy Taylor.

Reminiscing about how she came to Christ, Peters says, "About forty-seven years ago, on a carnival night, when many of my friends went dancing, I chose to go to church. That very same night the Lord came into my life."

Violet Brewster, wife of a Church of God pastor, influenced young Edith greatly, encouraging her to serve and take active positions in the church. She served on the ministerial council, in missionary societies, and as a teacher for more than forty years.

For six years, from 1980 to 1986, she served as pastor of the Villa Guadalupe Church. At the present, Reverend Edith Peters is president of the Ministerial Committee of Panama. She was that country's delegate to the Inter-American Conference in Santo Domingo in January 1988 and preached the closing sermon for the newly dedicated Church of God, in the Dominican Republic.

Daisy Taylor also grew up in Panama. The model life of her Christian mother guided her early years. In her church the services were only in English. Young Daisy felt the Holy Spirit burdening her to share the gospel with her Spanish neighbors and compatriots. She shared her concern with the governing body and they promptly sent her with a witnessing team to begin a mission in Villa Guadalupe. Thus began her ministry, which has continued for over twenty-six years.

For the last ten years, Sister Daisy and her husband, Brother Mendoza Taylor, have been outstanding pioneers of the Church of God in Colombia. They serve a dynamic congregation in Bogota and have established nine other congregations and trained many young leaders. The Taylors serve as inspiring and creative leaders to the continent.

Asked about any hardships or trials she had faced, Sister Daisy recalled an experience when she and Brother Mendoza first arrived in Colombia. The checks for their support from the Missionary Board had been delayed and all their funds had been depleted. "In a moment of desperation," she explained, "I sought God's help in prayer. Then the thought came to me that I could pawn my scissors. I went to the pawn shop, but the owner refused to accept them. He suggested, however, that I could leave my wedding ring. I left it and he gave me money so I could buy food for the family. When I told my husband the next day what had happened, he, too, went and pawned his wedding ring. With the money we paid some bills. Three weeks later the delayed checks arrived and we were able to reclaim our rings. That experience taught me a most valuable lesson. The Lord wished for us to depend exclusively on God for support. In my heart there awakened a new sensitivity for the needs of those around me and I have been able, since then, to minister to many human needs that surround me."

Puerto Rico

Claudina Ocasio de Rivas found the Lord when she was healed from an incurable illness. She has been a pastor for fifteen years in Tomas de Castro, the church she founded in 1973.

A deep burden to share the Lord with the youth and children of her *pueblo* led her into the ministry. The first years were full of hardship and crisis she recalls, because others did not want to accept her ministry. "But with much prayer and much love I overcame the obstacles," says Sister "Callita" as she is affectionately called by her children, friends, and parishioners. In Tomas del Castro, this woman reflects God's radiance and compassion.

Cuba

Carmen Martinez Romero writes, "I met the Lord when I was seven, in a little country church. I dreamed of being a missionary. I began preaching at seventeen and have done so ever since. I am now fifty-eight, and I hope to continue in the Lord's work until God calls me home where I will see God face to face and express my thanks and praises."

Rev. Carmen Martinez Romero has been president of the National Assembly of the Church of God in Havana, Cuba for two years. She has pastored two congregations: in Cascorro and Marianao. In addition to pastoring she has been a school teacher and has done extensive literacy work in Cuba. She has continued her training in various seminaries.

Recalling her greatest joys, she cites the conversion of her three sons and her youngest daughter's call to ministry. Other memorable moments were her ordination and her election to the presidency of the National Assembly.

Commenting about how she has been accepted, Hermana [Sister] Carmen says, "My brothers have had to accept my call because they realize it is of God. I did not seek it myself. I say to them, "If you're unhappy with women in ministry, complain to God. God called me." She further explains, "Now in Cuba, women are recognized as equal to men and they will just have to get used to this new order." Confidently this leader in Cuba relies on the Lord to bring about a great revival in Cuba and keep the churches dynamic and vibrant in their faith.

Hispanic Women Ministers in the United States

California

Mary Berthelsen was the pioneer leader of the Hispanic Church of God in Southern California. She and her husband began the Spanish work in Los Angeles in the early 1930s. She was an inspiration and encouragement to Juan Samuels in his work in Long Beach. She still played the piano at that church at the age of eighty-six!

Miriam Parisi serves as associate minister to her brother Juan Samuels. In her youth Miriam Samuels founded and pastored several of the first Churches of God in Cuba.

Texas

The Hispanic community in Texas has had two distinguished bilingual teachers who have been models of leadership and inspiration to young men and women pastors alike. Annie Tafolla and Sarah Tafolla Gerodetti played significant roles in the young Hispanic church movement in its early days. Their father, Mariano Tafolla was the pioneer founder of the Spanish Church of God in the USA. He began holding revivals along the Medina River in the late 1920s and 1930s. The congregations of San Antonio and Somerset grew out of these efforts.

Annie Tafolla graduated from Anderson University in 1930 and helped her father in all phases of the church's ministry. At the first meeting that Brother and Sister L.Y. Janes held in Corpus Christi, Annie was the speaker. She also served in the 1950s as the first and only woman editor to date of *La Trompeta*, the Spanish Church of God publications.

When asked why he stayed *true* to the Church of God during a period of prejudicial treatment by Anglo leaders, a

Hispanic pastor replied, "Sister Annie believed in me! That kept me going."

Affirmation and loving encouragement for the Tafolla sisters helped many young Hispanic male pastors survive the indifference and neglect they felt in the early years of the Spanish church in Texas.

Corpus Christi

In this city, the ministry of the Church of God began with Brother and Sister L.Y. Janes, after they returned from a missionary assignment in Panama.

Evelyn Janes Anderson reminiscing about the early days says that her mother, Una Janes, was the best teacher and greatest influence on her life. Other Hispanic pastors have fond memories of this saintly woman who encouraged them to enter the ministry.

Mother Janes held children's meetings in her living room. One day the house was packed with children. Her mother told Evelyn to take some of the younger children to the dining room and teach them. So Evelyn, knowing all the Bible stories, began at twelve to teach the little ones. Ever since, Sister Evelyn Anderson has been singing, writing, teaching, preaching, and publishing for the Spanish world.

Tons of tracts in Spanish, Portuguese, and English are printed at the Christian Triumph Company and mailed each year to national leaders in South and Central America.

Sister Anderson also directs a Spanish correspondence course to train and prepare leaders. As a teen-ager Evelyn had sought God's will for her life. She received Ephesians 4:12 as her confirmation. For a long time she did not understand her ministry, but forty years later, looking back over her life, she realizes the fulfillment of the scripture in her literature ministry.

Her life-long aspiration of being a missionary was suddenly realized in 1984 when she was invited to Peru to help begin the church in Caja de Agua. For fifty-two years Sister Evelyn has been the wife and companion to Noel Anderson.

Mexico

The best-known Hispanic woman leader in Mexico no doubt is Amelia Valdez Vazquez. In June of 1988, Anderson School of Theology bestowed on Sister Amelia its Distinguished Alumni Award.

Amelia has served the Church of God in Mexico for over thirty years. For twenty-six years she has taught in Saltillo, Mexico, at LaBuena Tierra Bible Institute (IBBT). No other Hispanic woman in our history has had such a consistent career as educator and pastor.

Amelia first came to know Christ through an invitation by Reverend Una Janes to a revival being held by Reverend A.T. Maciel in Corpus Christi in 1945. That same month Reverend L.Y. Janes baptized Amelia, her mother Andrea, and her sister Manuela.

She made a commitment to missionary service at a meeting in which Dr. J. Edgar Smith preached a sermon on consecration. Later three pioneers, D.W. Patterson, A.T. Maciel and L.Y. Janes were instrumental in her appointment to Mexico. In 1950, Amelia accepted the invitation from the Board of Church Extension and Home Missions to serve in Mexico. For four years she pastored the congregation in Nueva Leon and Coahuila. In the summer of 1951 she returned to New Mexico and planted the first Hispanic Church of God in Albuquerque.

For the next twenty-six years Amelia taught at the Bible Institute in Saltillo. For nine years, while teaching, she also pastored the congregation of San Antonio de las Alazanas. One of the highlights of her ministry was "seeing this struggling church come out of conflict and send nine young men and women to be trained at La Buena Tierra."

Reminiscing about the promising students she taught, she recalls Agustin: "He hardly knew how to read or write when he came to school. Now after graduating he has pastored three congregations, one of which he founded. In three years, the newly founded congregation grew from zero to 150 in membership. It gives me great delight to have had a part in training this young minister and many others." Upon her retirement in June of 1988, Amelia had served under the Missionary Board for seventeen years.

Amelia is married to Iamuel Vazquez, an active layperson and a great supporter of Amelia's ministry.

Florida

Hilaria and Ellsworth Palmer have pastored the Cuban Church of God in Miami for twenty-eight years. This church began in the living room of the Palmer home with the Cuban refugees' flight to Florida in 1960.

The Palmers have had an exceptional team ministry. Each person compliments the other's talents. Since 1940 this dedicated couple has served churches in Texas, California, Mexico, Cuba, and now Miami.

In addition to preaching on the radio and in the pulpit, teaching adults, counseling youth, Sister Hilaria has had a significant prayer ministry. Each Wednesday morning, women from the church and community gather to lift up to God the problems and needs of the neighborhood. Sister Hilaria tells stories of the ways the love and power of God has been experienced in these meetings and the many lives that have been transformed and homes changed.

Hilaria met Christ forty-three years ago when she was invited to help in a summer school at the Church of God in Matanzas, Cuba, her home. She says "I was very Catholic and I loved the Lord without knowing him. I had never read the Bible. It was a marvelous experience for me, reading the Word of God. Ever since I've taken it very seriously."

Hilaria met and married Ellsworth when he went to Cuba as a young missionary in the 1940s. Together they pastored the churches of Habana and Matanzas. Sister Palmer was ordained by the Cuban Assembly and her ministry has blessed and inspired many. Her constant source of strength has been Isaiah 26:3. She has suffered much criticism because of her preaching. Men felt she was usurping authority not rightfully hers, yet she has been faithful knowing that her call and authority comes from a loving God to whom she gives all the glory.

Oregon

Cati Perez-Scrivner left Texas as a young bride to live with Merle, her husband, in Portland, Oregon. Many Mexicans came to Oregon to pick fruit. In these new surroundings, Cati felt very burdened for these migrant workers. She says, "I saw my people with emptiness in their faces and I had a burning ache in my heart to tell them about Jesus. I knew my Savior could fill that emptiness."

Cati has now been pastor of the Ministerio Latino in the Rockwood Church of God in Portland, Oregon, for eight years. The congregation has grown to an attendance of 180 people. Cati's guiding theme is to "bless others." The Lord has beautifully met all the needs of this dynamic congregation. Discipling the laity is basic to Cati's approach to ministry. Recently the church purchased another bus to be able to bring more people to services from the migrant camps. The Latinos also installed a jacuzzi in the Rockwood Church baptistry so that the water would not be so cold for the many baptismal services that the Hispanics have.

Albuquerque

Shortly after their marriage, Cindy and Richard Mansfield moved to Corpus Christi, Texas, to work for an insurance company. Cindy and Richard were surprised by the hospitality of their neighbors, Felix and Silvia. "What impressed me most," says Cindy, "was the way God provided for their every need." Every night for a week this couple invited the Mansfields to dinner and after the meal, each time, they would ask their guests if they wanted to accept Christ, the Savior. After one week, Cindy and Richard both said yes! Holding hands the two couples knelt to pray. "That night God came and made a home in our hearts," continues Cindy, who will never forget that beautiful night. A few months later, God delivered Richard from alcohol and Cindy from narcotics she was beginning to take.

For a year Cindy and Richard became involved in many of the outreach ministries at the Iglesia de Dios in Corpus

Christi pastored by Reverend Gilberto Davila. Richard and Cindy are very talented musicians. They joined a group called "Blessings" and held concerts. Richard guided the prison ministries team and Cindy played the drums and worked with the drama and youth departments.

One night after watching "Fantasy Island," Cindy asked Richard what his fondest fantasy was. Richard replied, "To pastor my very own church!" One month later they received a call from the Board of Church Extension and Home Missions to become the pastors for the Albuquerque Hispanic Church of God.

The Mansfields have pastored this church now for seven years. They could write books about the experiences they have had with gang violence in the neighborhood and the miracles God has worked in the lives of families and young people.

Cindy has held leadership positions as Sunday school superintendent, preacher, coordinator of the Spiritual Life Department for the Women of the Church of God and last October was elected to be the National Spiritual Life Director of Women of the Church of God. Cindy is the first Hispanic-American woman to be elected to such a position of prominence.

To build self-esteem among the teen-agers of the Southside community, Cindy has organized a drum corps. They hope to "lead the parade for Jesus" in their city.

Two years ago Cindy had to undergo intensive jaw surgery. After five hours on the operating table, the surgeon ran into complications. He could not relocate the jaw in its original position. There was a sudden fear that Cindy might not survive because of major loss of blood. The head nurse, a Christian, pulled the surgical team aside and prayed a most fervent prayer that God would enable the surgeon to successfully reposition Cindy's jaw. Renewed, the surgeon went back and carefully moved the jaw again. He later explained, "It was like a special force pushing my hand." The jaw snapped into place. No wires were even needed to hold the corrected jaw in place. Cindy beams, "The Lord worked a beautiful miracle, and today the doctor is a Christian!"

Cindy and Richard feel a deep sense of calling and teamship in ministry and know that Romans 8:28 is true! God does work in all things for good.

Washington, D.C.

After hours of prayer one night last October, Tina Cotto made a pledge to God that she would study for the ministry. She dreams of getting a doctoral degree in counseling and of doing intensive Bible study. "I have this dream to share Christ and I want to have the credentials to work in institutions," Tina says. In their Hispanic church in Washington, D.C., David and Tina stress making converts into disciples. For the Concilio they both dream of having it grow in effectiveness, love, and outreach. (David Cotto is currently the president of the Concilio.)

When asked where she first came to know Christ, Tina answered, "At a little church across from the place where I used to disco. My mother's bowling partner invited me there. The pastor took my name and kept calling. He even sent a young lady to take me to Bible studies. I had been bound by drugs, but one night in 1980, God made a marvelous change in my life!"

Her pastors, Harold and Jackie Harrison, were the most influential persons in young Tina's *walk* with Christ. "They were my spiritual godparents. . . . All they said, they lived. That gave me hope. There was also, in them, such a sense of urgency and deep yearning to share Christ. That impressed me," says Tina.

Later, when Tina met Sister Hattie Downer, she was utterly fascinated by this saintly woman's radiance and joy. Sister Hattie, a wise leader, discerned Tina's gifts for ministry and encouraged Tina to share, preach, and witness in the church in Brooklyn.

One summer at a youth camp she met David Cotto. "I fell in love with that man's spirit," recalls Tina, brightly.

In September of 1982 they were married. "I have been so blessed," says Tina. "David, my beloved husband, encourages my potential. We have two beautiful daughters, and I have come to know that in Christ I am somebody! My whole being blesses God when someone is healed or finds Christ or when a woman understands her self-worth."

Kingsville, Texas

"It wasn't until I started serving in various ministries of the church in Corpus that I began to realize that God was preparing me to become a pastor. In 1986, at the Hispanic Church of God Convention, I was assured of my calling," says Aggie Villarreal, founder and pastor of the new congregation in Kingsville, Texas.

For nine years Aggie was active in Pastor Gilberto Davila's congregation. Her pastor encouraged her to begin the Kingsville work when she shared her burden to start a church in her hometown. John, her husband, supports Aggie's ministry completely and directs the music. Ana, her seventeen-year-old daughter, teaches the children in Sunday school.

Aggie's favorite Scripture is Proverbs 3:5, "Trust in the Lord with all your heart and lean not on your own understanding. In all your ways acknowledge him and he will direct your paths."

One of the significant moments of her ministry occurred one Sunday at the Corpus Christi church after she had preached the morning sermon. As she gave an altar call, many persons came forward. "I especially noticed one family whose members were all crying and hugging each other," says Aggie. After prayer, the father stood up and told the congregation what had happened. Back in California (from where the people had come), the father had had an argument with his son. The boy had run away and they did not know where he was.

This family had come to Corpus Christi to visit relatives and had come to the church, not knowing that their son was in the audience also. They had met and forgiven each other at the altar, and now were planning to take their son back home. In that moment, Aggie had a marvelous experience of the transforming, healing love of God in the reunion of a family.

Brooklyn, New York

Last year, Rosita Dominguez, a young woman from El Salvador, began to hold Bible studies in her apartment. Rosita came from Reverend Tito Ayala's church in El Salvador and had a great burden to share Christ with the Hispanic community. Recently Rosita has begun working with Sister Hattie Downer in her Brooklyn neighborhood. Rosita's ministry is very promising and she needs our love, prayers, and support as she tries to be a witness for Christ. Surely New York is a ripe mission field with over a million Puerto Ricans and Hispanics.

A new day is dawning on the Hispanic horizon. In both Americas, women are awakening and responding to Christ's call to witness, love, heal, reconcile, bind up wounds, feed the hungry, and proclaim the Light of the World!

Dondeena Caldwell

Dondeena lived four years in Syria and Egypt while her parents, William and Vada Fleenor, were missionaries there; then she lived in Anderson, Indiana, attending the public schools and college. She received her B.A. degree with majors in Bible and English from Anderson University, and her Masters degree in Spanish Literature and Language from the University of the Americas in Mexico City, Mexico.

The first pastorate for Dondeena and Maurice Caldwell was the Hispanic congregation, Belvedere Church of God in Los Angeles, California. She assisted in the founding of the Bible Institute in Saltillo, Mexico, La Buena Tierra; and the Bible Institute in Curitiba, Brazil, Boa Terra. Dondeena has served as a career missionary most of her life. She served in Mexico for eleven years and in Brazil for eight years. She has been a linguist, teacher, translator, and editor.

The Brazilian women have found their voice through training and leadership provided by Dondeena. The young people have been trained in her classes of Christian Education and music, and the lay people have been guided and taught through the publications La Trompeta *(Spanish counterpart of* Vital Christianity*), and* A Trombeta, *the Portuguese magazine. She also edited the bulletin* O Desafio *for the Nation Women's Society of Brazil. Another major project was the translation and publication of Spanish and Portuguese hymn books.*

Dondeena has served as Associate Secretary for Women of the Church of God. She now serves as Director of Missions Education and editor of Church of God Missions *magazine.*

Chapter 6:

Women in Cross-Cultural Missions
of the Church of God

Dondeena Caldwell

The press clanked as the master printer operated it with her foot. Ruth Murray was turning out Sunday school helps for the Church of God in Kenya, devotional materials, school books, song sheets, and eventually a hymnbook of three hundred songs. She often would illustrate the materials with hand-drawn pictures.

Gertrude Kramer and Mabel Baker worked closely with Murray in the early 1900s. They provided the translated materials for her to print. Kramer also translated the New Testament into the dialect of the Olunyore tribe, ofttimes with her children at her side clamoring for attention. Baker made the spelling uniform and revised the translation into more idiomatic language of the tribe, and in 1938 the American Bible Society printed the Kramer/Baker translation of the New Testament.

These women were some of the pioneers in the work of the Church of God in Kenya. Their contribution went beyond denominational boundaries and helped to spread the Good News to all of the Olunyore tribe. Their call to follow Christ also went beyond traditional expectations, that of marrying a committed Christian and being supportive of *his* ministry through homemaking and raising a family.

Kramer, Baker, Murray, and many women before and after them have used their spiritual gifts to be cross-cultural missionaries. They responded to the call to proclaim the gospel to people of another culture. Women such as these assist women in other nations who have accepted Jesus Christ and work in partnership with them. They live and work with persons having behavorial patterns and traditional ways of life different from their own; such is the work of cross-cultural missions.

The first woman of the Church of God to be a part of a cross-cultural mission is remembered only as "Mrs." She and her husband, John Rupert, went from the United States to England in 1892 when the Church of God reformation movement was twelve years old. Historical records have left her nameless, faceless, and with no trace of her contribution as a missionary.

By 1911, five more women left to accompany their husbands overseas, yet we have no record of the wives' names. George and Mrs. Martin went to England and Scotland in 1891. In 1904, George and Mrs. Bailey went to India. Then in 1908 another George took his unknown-to-us wife to Trinidad: George and Mrs. Pye. We could conjecture that these three men named George seldom, if ever, called their wives by their first names, referring to them only as 'wife,' as in "wife and I are leaving for missionary service."

In the early years of missionary outreach, inadequate records can be understandable; but nineteen and twenty years after the first missionary left the United States border for Mexico, two women were still nameless, faceless, and with no trace of their cross-cultural contributions. Edward and Mrs. Reedy went to Trinidad in 1911. The following year Robert and Mrs. Springer went to Russia and Switzerland.

Even after the formal organization of the Missionary Board of the Church of God in 1909, three married women who accompanied their husbands on missionary assignments were nameless: Mrs. Samuel Joiner (Kenya, 1922), Mrs. William Conkis (Egypt, 1933), and Mrs. George Dallas (Egypt, 1933). No men's names seem to have been lost for the records, neither were any names of single women missionaries forgotten. The acceptance of women as persons in their own right, rather than as extensions of their husbands, was and still is part of the problem of identity.

One former missionary to Kenya said, "I was looked on by most of the male missionaries as just a wife and young mother. It was frustrating to be considered only a missionary's wife. We both felt called, commissioned, and sent. It seemed unfair that the single females were considered to be missionaries, but we wives were there mainly for support."

That sense of call from God to serve in a cross-cultural setting was expressed in a survey of former and present missionary women. Out of thirty-six responses, only three indicated that they went overseas because of their husband's call. More than half of the women felt called during their youth, and some as young as six years of age. Many had parents with a global consciousness. The call came after exposure to missionaries, reading missionary books, or working with women's missionary groups. Others were challenged through Student Volunteers, Tri-S (Student Summer Service of Anderson University), and Religious Emphasis Weeks on campuses.

Twyla Ludwig felt God's call to go to Africa (Kenya, 1927-49) even before her husband John was converted. Ruth Shotton, who served in Mexico, Panama, and Venezuela says, "I was uneducated, had a husband who had been a Christian only a few years, and had four children. God made it clear to me my calling, 'The Spirit of the Lord is upon *me*, because he hath anointed *me* to preach the gospel' " (Luke 4:18-19).

This strong sense of calling has sent women, both single and married, into many countries of the world with the gospel. Most have been involved in the helping professions, such as nursing, teaching, and social work where demands and responsibilities correspond to those of a home. Not all women aspire to leadership positions, but many women do possess the gift of administration or preaching. All of these women can be accepted as translators, teachers, administrators, medical workers, or preachers, not because of their gender but because they are using their spiritual gifts within the authority of the church.

Georgia Harkness says that the energy and productivity of womanhood are still imprisoned to a degree by men and by women themselves: "The church has not challenged women to recognize their God-given gifts, encouraged them to fully use their talents, or helped them to gain a mature sense of personhood" (Harkness 1972, 13).

In spite of a lack of encouragement at times, women in the Church of God have made and are making an invaluable contribution to the church and the world. In fact, the majority of missionaries sent out by the church has been and continues to be female. More than 115 single women make up this great host of cross-cultural missionaries, some serving only one year and others for as long as thirty-nine years (Mabel Baker and Josephine McCrie).

The first single woman to go as a missionary was Lena Shoffner. She went to England in 1893 and worked for two years. Nine more singles followed her example in the following decade, going to Mexico, India, Trinidad, Russia, and Jamaica. Outstanding among them was Josephine McCrie, who spent thirty-nine years in India.

Between 1910 and 1920, thirteen single women were called to serve in Denmark, Sweden, China, Syria, Barbados, Trinidad, India, Kenya, and Japan. Among them was Nellie Laughlin, who was working with F.G. Smith, his wife, Birdie, and Bessie Hittle in Syria. When World War I erupted, the missionaries found themselves in enemy territory and were advised to leave. Even though the other three left, Nellie chose to stay. All contact was cut with her by 1917. She managed to find enough food to keep herself and a small group of believers alive. "She spent her time indoctrinating these young converts in biblical truth. Nellie had become a full-time missionary and was the only missionary of the Church of God in that entire area" (Crose 1983, 43).

Following the war she made the decision to move the work of the church from the small village of Schweifat to the city of Beirut, the kind of a decision usually made by the male leadership of a church. Nellie later served in Egypt until her retirement.

Mabel Baker arrived in Kenya in 1914 and spent thirty-nine years involved in many aspects of the work there. She became the chairperson and treasurer of the African Assembly while John and Twyla Ludwig were on furlough. At the same time she was educational secretary for all the village schools. She managed the bookshop, translated, printed, and supplied Sunday school material for the villages. She was also treasurer for the girls' school. The younger Africans declared that she had a greater Olunyore vocabulary than any of them (Williams 1986, 99).

In the decade of the 1920s, single women went to Ireland, India, Japan, Kenya, and Jamaica. Among them were Edith Young, who spent thirty-seven years in Jamaica; Naomi Allan, who spent thirty-six years in Ireland; and Mona Moors, who spent thirty-three years in India. Young taught full time at Jamaica Bible Institute until her retirement. Allan's contribution to Kingdom work was to edit the *British Gospel Trumpet*. When Moors first went to India, she was put in charge of a home for boys in Cuttack. Later she managed the Shelter for girls, along with Indian sisters, Sonat and Nolini Mundul, giving most of her time to the care and education of the girls.

Ellen High joined Mona Moors in Cuttack in 1937 and worked in India for twenty-one years. Other single women went to Cuba, Kenya, and Egypt during the thirties. One of them, Lima Lehmer, spent twenty-six years at the hospital and school in Kima, Kenya. Besides teaching Bible to the women of various villages, she and Jewell Hall taught weekly Bible classes at Mwihila for pastors who had no formal training. Since her retirement she has published a book about missionary life in East Africa, *Walking in Missionary Shoes* (Williams 1986).

Fourteen single women were sent by the Missionary Board in the 1940s to work in cross-cultural missions. They went to Grand Cayman, Kenya, China, Cuba, Jamaica, Antigua, and St. Kitts. After spending a year in Antigua, Wilhelmina Fraser continued to work with the church in St. Kitts for twenty-eight years. Three women who went to Kenya during that decade remained for over twenty years: Jewell Hall, Irene Engst, and Lydia Hanson worked for twenty-eight, twenty-seven, and twenty-four years respectively. Their medical and teaching skills brought healing and training to an untold number of people. Jewell Hall opened a teacher training facility in Mwihila. Engst wrote, "I helped get the Mwihila medical work started by holding a dispensary first outdoors and then in a small building. I helped start the women's work in Kenya, taught in the Teacher Training Center, and did general mission work."

For the next two decades (1950-69), the majority of all single women involved in missions went to Kenya as nurses. Only seven out of thirty-seven went elsewhere: to Barbados, Grand Cayman, Trinidad, Japan, and Hong Kong. The three women with the longest tenure in Kenya for this period are Edna Thimes with nineteen years, Velma Schneider with sixteen, and Vera Martin with fifteen. Through Thimes's efforts and the practice of preventive medicine, such as vaccinations and immunizations, the cases of polio and other childhood diseases were diminished in the Kima/Mwihila area. Martin was on the Medical Council of Kenya, which included all government and mission hospitals. She sat on the licensing board for four years to review nurses who entered the colony for registration. Because of her contacts, the Church of God in Kenya received many considerations, such as free food for the needy and free medications.

During the history of Church of God missions, forty-six percent of all single missionaries have gone to Kenya. By the early to mid-1980s the largest number of missionaries ever were sent to Kenya, and most of them were women. About one-third of the total number of missionaries were involved in educational work, one-third in the medical program, and one-third in direct church-related work. The British colonial government provided financial grants to Christian missions involved in education and medical services to help the country develop more rapidly. This gave more than the usual number of women with such skills an opportunity to serve overseas.

Kenya again headed the list for single missionaries in the 1970s and 1980s. Other women used their skills as teachers, for the most part, in Japan, Mexico, Brazil, Hong Kong, and Taiwan. A trend for shorter terms of missionary service emerged. Most going overseas during these two decades gave three to five years of their lives as teachers or nurses, rather than to become "career" missionaries.

Not everyone is called to be a "career" missionary, nor are there as many opportunities for single women to dedicate the rest of their lives in such work. Often countries close their doors to religious workers, both single and married. As the national church of each country matures and grows, it finds leadership among its own people, usually among the men.

Carroll, Hargrove, and Lummis say,

> Changes in the status and visibility of women in churches have been in response to internal phases within the life cycle of religious movements. Women have usually been permitted freedom of expression and exercise of leadership in the first stage of the movement, or "charismatic phase."
>
> As the movement becomes older and larger, it enters its "consolidation and organization phase" in which women are absorbed into a system dominated by men and not allowed much autonomy of expression, organization, or decision-making" (Carroll 1982).

This is one of the reasons fewer single women are involved as leaders in cross-cultural missions today. The trend toward shorter terms of missionary service in the last few decades is probably a reflection of the trend in our society. Choosing a career in our culture has traditionally been perceived as a once-in-a-lifetime decision. Statistics now show that those who enter the job market in the 1980s can be expected to change jobs between twelve to fifteen times during their working lives (Caldwell 1988, 5-8).

In spite of such trends, single and married women are still called to mission and find a multitude of ways and opportunities to fulfill the Great Commission. At times, though, the married woman is at a disadvantage, especially if her husband "jealously guards his *role* as the leader and decision maker," as one missionary's wife commented. Most husbands consider their wives to be team members, but the national church leaders often do not perceive the wives to be of equal value in carrying out the Great Commission.

Just how are women as missionaries and co-leaders perceived by their male colleagues and national workers? The response to the survey question was varied. Most of the single women felt equally valued and involved. More wives than singles had ambivalent feelings about their worth and acceptance. Granted, both married or singles must "earn" the respect from their colleagues, but the way a woman feels about her contribution and self-worth as a missionary often is determined by her personality, training, husband/wife relationship, and the opportunities she is afforded to use her God-given talents. Another factor that helps to determine whether equal partnership in mission can exist for women is the attitude toward them in the local culture (Caldwell March 1988, 8).

"My husband was looked upon as the one having more experience," was the response from one woman who had worked in Kenya. From Japan a wife wrote, "The national church leaders would probably take my husband's opinion over mine." And from Bolivia, where women are to be observers rather than leaders, Barbara Miller, a licensed minister, says, "I relate well to Bolivian brethren, but am not considered an equal to my husband when it comes to missionary duties and responsibilities." On the other hand, Ruth Shotton tells about her experiences in Mexico and

Panama: "In Mexico I worked 'under cover' or 'behind the scenes' because of 'machismo' in the masculine society. In Panama I was more openly accepted, especially by the black culture. This was a carry-over from the favorable acceptance of their own women as leaders. On the Kuna Yala Islands, the Kuna Indians have a matriarchal society. Their male leaders sometimes turned to me before they did to my husband."

While women in missions are respected, some feel more acceptance than others. "I am respected," says a missionary from Tanzania, "but I am not taken into confidence." "I am the missionary's wife," says another woman, "not the missionary," even though she is licensed. "I was viewed by the men as a 'girl,' an unmarried woman, but fully valued by the women of Kenya," reported another. Many women expressed the fact that the national leaders expected more from them than they did from their own women. Others have felt uncomfortable when put on a pedestal.

Kay Critser wrote from Tanzania: "I am viewed by the nationals as a foreigner who has come with expertise which they can use. I have found that when women have proven that they have abilities other than what society has decreed they should have, they are respected by men as long as they in return respect them."

The acceptance of women in positions of leadership has changed over the years, not only among missionaries. Retha Shultz states, "In Kenya many areas exist, certainly in the home, where the man is 'king.' In the church the men are by far the most prominent. The interesting fact is that men are realizing that the women are the ones with a tremendous ability to manage the affairs of the household and also of the church. Even the government appointed women instead of men to be in charge of some of the programs which had been set up."

Jenny Schwieger adds, "Today many women are in leadership roles in the Kenyan church and are listened to and serve on many decision-making committees. The role of the missionary has changed from leader or 'all-knowing one' to advisor and co-worker. The 'co-worker' response to women missionaries has come with the leadership of Marilyn Farag who always made sure that the decision of the Africans was acted upon, not her decision."

Most women feel valued if they work within the confines of the cross-cultural situation, which usually means working with women.

Such a woman is Frances Clark who recalls her work in East Pakistan: "I was a full partner with my husband, in charge primarily in the home, with women, children, health, and home training—areas impossible for men to enter. I did not feel mine was a second class role in any sense, nor was I encouraged to feel so."

The most frustrating experience though is to feel that within our own North American culture, women still are considered to be less than co-workers with their husbands and male colleagues. One former missionary wrote, "The political structure of the church, missions, and government were always kept in male hands. I wrote letters to the executive officers of the Missionary Board and signed my husband's name, because I knew they would be dealt with as of greater significance. I practiced this all fifteen years of our relationship with the Board. I felt it was a necessary procedure to reach desired goals."

Women want to be accepted as an integral part of the decision-making and work involvement as missionaries. That their responsibilities often are limited to women and children might at first seem to be unjust and less productive than possible. "Don't slight women's ministries," says Mary Lou Walls, missionary to Venezuela. "That should be an integral part of a woman as missionary. She is the female example and leader."

Since women make up more than half of the world's population, they should be the recipients of at least half of our time and efforts. Who would be more aware and sympathetic of women and their needs than a woman of God who is striving to serve those who suffer injustice and deprivation? As missionaries work with women, they discover those who are dynamic agents for change in our world. Women's "existential link to life fosters attitudes in them that are life preserving and life enhancing. Wherever women engage in processes of self-dignification and join forces with others, they embody courage and hope and become agents for change" (Garcia 1987, 30).

Such change came to the women in the Church of God in Brazil. In 1971, a local pastor announced the annual business meeting to be held at the end of the service. As was the custom in every church, he ended the announcement saying, "All women and children will be excused." Seventy percent of those present filed out without saying a word. That all changed after the women were given a chance to develop their leadership abilities through a local and national women's organization. Their efficient business meetings and successful budgetary goals, as well as their increased knowledge of the Bible and missions education was a challenge to the General Ministerial Assembly. Today the women in the church in Brazil are accepted as valued partners because someone saw value in them and in "women's work" performed by missionaries.

The church in several countries has been enhanced through the work of organized women's groups, work that brings self-dignification and development to women. Missionaries in Japan, Jamaica, Mexico, Brazil, Venezuela, Kenya, Egypt, the Caribbean, and other areas have lifted the hopes and skills of women through the unique contributions of such organizations.

Women of the Church of God in North America also are deeply involved in cross-cultural mission as they support projects to relieve hunger, to educate, to build necessary facilities all around the world. To mention all that has been done through these women would be impossible, but a few examples follow. The hospital and first missionary residence at Mwihila were built with funds from Women of the Church of God. They also provided the money to build the first church in Mexico City. Many leaders from other countries have received scholarships from the women for advanced training. This indirect cross-cultural assistance strengthens what missionary women are doing while serving overseas.

Most women feel they are or have been an integral part in decision-making among their missionary colleagues, although not always in the cross-cultural setting. A few younger wives found themselves "filling in the gaps" and pressured into emergency and women's work when they felt capable and willing to do more. That was not the case of Edna Thimes in Kenya who reported that she (a single missionary) was involved in decision-making in the General Assembly, the Executive Council of the same, the Board of Christian Education, the college and hospital of the Church of God, as well as the Friends' Hospital and Anglican Hospital in the community. The church in Kenya even ordained her.

Ruth Sanderson left Kenya in 1958, two years before Edna Thimes arrived. Sanderson's experience while there shows some of the changes that took place after she left. She says, "Missionaries held staff meetings, and I had a vote. However, most of the men were on most of the committees. All of the men were ordained, no matter what their previous occupation or training. None of the women were ordained. They tended to do 'women's work' except in emergencies."

Retha Shultz, who served with her husband in Trinidad, added, "In some areas I was an integral part. However, when it came to the official committees of the church, usually I was not an officer or involved officially." She and others would agree with Roberta Hestenes who said, "I was encouraged to share my faith actively while always granting to men the formal positions within our church" (Hestenes 1988).

The woman's role in cross-cultural mission, especially among married women, often has been one of taking the back seat and only indirectly influencing the drivers. Called 'pillow diplomacy' in the world, it nonetheless is one way women influence the decisions made among the church's leaders. To be ordained is no guarantee that a woman will be accepted as a 'driver' in the church, as is the case of Barbara Miller in Bolivia. Culture often dictates. Add to that a woman's acceptance of her limited opportunity to serve.

Phyllis Kinley, who has been in Japan with her husband since 1958, observes that at the time of her calling to cross-cultural mission women were not challenged to become ordained ministers. Instead she chose to marry a minister and share in his work. Since her husband Philip is the director of Tamagawa Seigakuin Girl's School, she has been doing much of the pastoral work of the Hagiyama Church and much of the actual evangelism and counseling for the past fifteen years. It was either that or close the church for lack of leadership.

If Phyllis Kinley had gone to Japan as an ordained minister, today she would automatically be a member of the *Renmei*, the Japanese Association of the Church of God, and also be a part of the pastors' decision-making body. "Because I am not ordained," she says, "I cannot baptize persons, conduct communion services, or pronounce the benediction. I can do almost anything else, including preaching when my husband is away." (He still is considered to be the legal pastor of the church, even though she does most of the work.) Her inability to perform certain pastoral tasks, as well as be a part of the *Renmei* and pastors' group stems not so much from her gender as from her lack of ordination. In this case, ordination means power because the decisions of the church are made by the ordained.

Still, women continue to serve in cross-cultural missions, ordained or not and the married one works for little or no pay. Her role has largely been defined by her husband's assignment. She is expected to support and adapt to his vocation. A lack of recognition affects single women missionaries to some degree, but is even more characteristic of missionary wives whose husbands' work is often seen to be the 'real' mission work. Even though both partners of a missionary couple are considered to be missionaries, usually a single check is made out in the husband's name, and only he accrues Social Security, retirement, and other benefits.

The missionary wife goes through the same application process as her husband. They both receive orientation, often considered to be inadequate, and are included in the commissioning service. Usually the wife has no particular assignment. She must find her own avenue of service. She is neither required nor pressured to do mission work, other than çaring for her home and family (Bowers 1984).

With little direction and even less preparation, the significant contribution that women have made is a miracle. Ann Smith says that she knew nothing of cross-cultural skills before going to Japan in 1951. Ruth Kilmer states, "We had no orientation in mission work, methods, or even the history of the station and culture to which we were being sent. Some things we learned the hard way." Norma Borden suggests that the Missionary Board do more to equip missionaries and give them more emotional support and chances for spiritual refreshment.

Equipped or not, women in cross-cultural situations find unique ways to meet the needs of the community and the church while at the same time serving as the traditional Sunday school teacher, hostess, care-giver, or support system for the more visible leaders. The traditional careers for women—secretary, teacher, or nurse—are utilized on the mission field, but often take on added leadership responsibilities. Several women have used their skills as bookkeepers for schools, hospitals, mission staffs, or assemblies. Margaret Tiesel taught bookkeeping methods to church treasurers in the West Indies. Bernie Dean helped to get a business department started at Ardenne High School in Jamaica.

The contribution of women to education, both secular and religious, has no equal. Nina Ratzlaff started the Triple C School in Grand Cayman which still is doing well. Later she taught Christian Education at the Jamaica Bible Institute. Many other women have been the guiding force to educate children, train teachers, and create or translate curricula and books for use in the classrooms and the church. At the same time some have had to teach their own children at home.

Lester Crose writes about Nellie Olson who organized not one but two educational institutions. "In 1928, Nellie Olson, feeling the need for a better-trained ministry, opened the Jamaica Bible Institute. She observed immediately that most of the students had not yet completed secondary school, and so the very next year she opened a high school department at the institute" (Crose 1983, 84). The new department became Ardenne High School and still is one of the outstanding secondary schools in Jamaica.

Women have been involved in the planning for and teaching in several other Bible Institutes. Retha Shultz helped organize the Bible School in Trinidad where she also taught. Later she was a teacher in two other Bible schools. Mary Butz was the spark and work force to establish the Bible Institute in Peru. Dondeena Caldwell helped to organize, direct, and teach in Bible schools in Mexico and Brazil.

Another important contribution of women to cross-cultural missions is their teaching of music and theory. True, people of every culture have always been able to sing and play indigenous musical instruments, but often they have had no written music, nor could they read it if it were available. Women more than men have been the teachers of piano, voice, and music theory.

At the VII World Conference held in 1983 in Nairobi, Kenya, East Africa, the executive officer of the Church of God, Byrum Makokha, introduced several outstanding choirs from our churches of Kenya. He said, "We Africans have always been able to sing. We have a good sense of rhythm, but it took the missionary to teach us how to sing in harmony." Much of the credit can be taken by people like Fern Ludwig Rogers who organized the annual Music Festivals of Kenya and Grace Donohew who translated and printed *Waves of Devotion*, a hymnbook, into the Luyia language.

In Brazil, music played a minor role in the church. Sermons provided spiritual validity to the services. After missionary women trained choirs and musicians, the women asked the all-male ministerial assembly to allow the choir to perform a cantata during the annual convention. One pastor's response was, "Do you mean there will be no sermon? How can that be spiritual?" Needless to say, more people came to the altar for prayer after the cantata than after any sermon during the convention, and music is now used as a dynamic witness to the church and the community.

Music as a ministry has been only one way women serve while involved in other work. Several women have drawn plans for dormitories, homes, and a hospital. They have worked side by side with male colleagues to construct the buildings, laying bricks and placing tiles on the roofs. A few have even supervised the construction of buildings.

Other contributions from women in cross-cultural missions includes working with refugees, prostitutes, and the mentally and physically handicapped. Unique was Glenna Yutzy's work: she operated a short-wave radio three times a day to other stations. Kay Critser reports working with the people in Tanzania to plant an eight-acre field of corn.

Few women, though, within the last few years have been given the opportunity to use their administrative skills. Two exceptions are Dorothy Sharp and Magaline Hoops. Sharp was surprised that she, instead of her husband, was asked to be the mission's interim secretary-treasurer in Kenya, and he was quite supportive of her in that position. From others she was given the impression that no major decision was to be made during her one year's responsibilities.

After the death of Roy Hoops, his wife Magaline became the mission secretary-treasurer for Tanzania and served in that position for three years. Later she moved to Kenya and in 1988 she was asked to become the mission secretary-treasurer, a responsibility she still assumes. Because of her position, she is included on several committees with the national leadership of the church in Kenya. Occasionally she has had trouble with male egos among her colleagues who are unaccustomed to being answerable to a woman.

Added to the women serving overseas are those doing cross-cultural work here at home. These women deserve recognition and empowerment. Lillie McCutcheon says, "It is inconsistent when there is little controversy over women who are commissioned to difficult mission fields but are not on the other hand esteemed eligible for ordination in the homeland" (McCutcheon 1980).

Juanita Bean, a public health nurse in Fairbanks, Alaska, is such a woman. She joins Indians and Eskimos on a live radio program, testifying and urging those listening to give their hearts and lives to the Lord. Besides her work at the clinic, she plays the organ for church, grieves with those who have lost a loved one, counsels and prays with those having marital problems. In one month alone she had Indian guests in her home who needed a place to stay while in Fairbanks for twenty-five nights.

Esther Bailey and her husband Earl founded the work among the Sioux Indians and established the Inter-Cultural Center in Scottsbluff in 1954. In 1973, Ida Hawk and Ben Clown Horse nominated Esther Bailey for "Mother of the Year" for her work among the Indians, a testimony to the value they placed on her work.

When Marge Williams's husband Adam died in 1978 their congregation voted unanimously for her to continue the work he was doing as pastor of the Church of God in the Tulalip reservation and as a counselor for drug addicts and alcoholics. She conducts weekly meetings and does follow-up in the homes to teach the Bible.

After ten years of her ministry, she has a congregation that includes sixty recovering alcoholics who praise her efforts to get at the number one problem of the Indians— tragedies related to drug and alcohol abuse.

In a chapel service during her senior year at Asbury College, Naomi Randall heard a woman mission worker and four mountain girls tell of their life in the coal mining areas of the Appalachian Mountains. Naomi wrote in her diary, "God spoke to my heart and so definitely. I know he wants me in the mountains. God has shown me my life's work" (Randall n.d.).

After completing her Masters degree at Ohio State University in 1939, she went to the mountains of Eastern Kentucky to minister. Up and down the coal mining valleys she rode the train, stopping in one community after another to teach Sunday school classes, to conduct Vacation Bible Schools, and to direct youth meetings. In many of these communities she preached and helped to raise funds for the new church buildings. Naomi was not ordained so she never assumed the role of pastor.

After becoming Associate Secretary of the National Board of Church Extension and Home Missions, she helped organize the American Indian Council and the Spanish Concilio.

Whether at home or overseas, women can and should be used more effectively in the leadership of cross-cultural missions. The problem comes in putting them to work. If they have not been encouraged to develop and grow, all too often they feel like the unfaithful servant in Matthew 25:14-30 who hid his talent. A great deal of conscious, and even subconscious, feeling exists on the part of most men about women leading, says Ted Engstrom. He adds, "Women need the encouragement and acceptance of men and other women to become all that God would have them to be. Many of them would surprise themselves, as well as their colleagues, at how well they might carry out an executive position" (Engstrom 1988).

That women as missionaries are seldom recognized as executives or thought to be capable of making top level decisions is reflected in what they are asked to do while on home assignment or after leaving their mission responsibilities. Only Ann Smith and Gwendolyn Massey have served on the administrative staff of the Missionary Board, and few have been elected to membership on the Board. The majority of former and present missionary women surveyed responded that the church makes little use of their skills and experience when they return home. Said one, "The church does not use my skills in any special way. I am usually asked only the questions that pertain to the women's daily life. The wife and children seem to be on exhibit more than contributing to the mission enterprise." Another added, "It is possible that the American Church does not really value the experience and skills of the missionary woman upon her return. Skills of knowledge, insight, culture, and language are often ignored on the part of American society because they are unimportant to them."

Recognizing the tension between respecting the values in a local culture, either overseas or at home, and the need for change, we still face another problem if we are to utilize the potential for leadership that women possess. It is evident in the title to an article written by Carole Maines: "Missionary

Wives: Underused Asset." She asks, "What will happen if mission boards maintain the status quo, neglecting the professional development of their missionary wives, and allowing a major percentage of them to remain largely uninvolved?" (Maines 1983).

Most married women find involvement and consider themselves a member of a team, but none receive benefits or comparable pay for comparable work. Consideration should be given to the new role emerging in some mission groups, that of the 'parallel worker,' a wife who has distinct work and pay within the same organization that employs her husband. She may even have full-time employment unrelated to her husband's assignment. Ideally, "both husband and wife are involved in creating a nurturing home environment, and both are enabled to find fulfillment in the stewardship of their abilities and gifts" (Bowers 1984, 8).

The hope of women in cross-cultural missions is that one day the mission of the church will be holistic. That implies the construction of a practical theology that will lay the foundation for a new way in which women can use their gifts and talents in their involvements in the church. Our mission goes beyond the 'four walls' of a congregation. Our work takes on breadth and depth that reaches beyond a small circle of women. Our ministry takes place in the multifaceted testimonial work of all believers (1 Peter 2:9) in carrying out of the Great Commission. Our biblical-theological criterion is based on the conviction that both female and male are created in God's image. If we all are created in God's likeness, we participate in God's way of being. We are co-participants with God in the re-creation of humanity in reconciliation, solidarity, and community (Garcia 1987, 32).

The fact remains that without women's skills of servant leadership and their sensitivity to the call of God, without their effectual financial support of mission causes coupled with their disciplined study of the world and its needs, the cross-cultural mission efforts of the church would be decimated. The time has come not only to recognize the vital contribution that women have made and are making to cross-cultural mission, but to accept, to train, and to empower them to take the gospel to every race, to every place, and to every generation.

Ruth M. Smith

Ruth M. Smith is an ordained minister of the Church of God serving the church in Glen Burnie, Maryland. She holds a Master of Science degree in Natural Science from Muhlenberg College, Allentown, Pennsylvania, and a Master of Divinity degree from Anderson University School of Theology, Anderson, Indiana. She is presently working on a Certificate Program at Shalem Institute for Spiritual Formation, Washington D. C.

Ruth has served on the Anderson University Board of Trustees, and has worked with national and state ministerial assemblies. She has served as coordinator for ecumenical services in the Glen Burnie, Maryland area.

She has published articles in Vital Christianty.

June D. Strickland

June Strickland is an ordained minister of the Church of God serving the church in Nacogdoches, Texas. She attended public schools in Ohio, then studied at Gulf Coast Bible College in Houston, Texas, graduating with a Bachelor of Theology degree.

She has served as associate pastor and as pastor for several churches in Texas. She has been guest speaker for conventions, youth camps, and prayer retreats. She has also served on state and national ministerial councils.

Vivian W. Moore

Vivian Moore is an ordained minister and a dedicated educator. She holds a Masters degree in Education from Washington University, St. Louis, Missouri. She was named "Teacher of the Year" in 1976, was listed in "Who's Who in Black America" and in "Community Leaders and Noteworthy Americans."

In addition to planting new churches, she was founder of The Childrens Academy, Dell Wood, Missouri, and co-founder of the St. Louis Academy for Children. She has administered programs for gifted, co-authored curriculum for low achievers, and supervised teacher training.

Vivian has served on many civic committees in St. Louis and Chicago. She has been a Coordinator and consultant for many black programs for career development. She is guest soloist and speaker for various churches in the St. Louis area.

Chapter 7:

Contemporary Profiles of
Women in Ministry

Introduction

Soon it will be two thousand years since the women and men who followed Jesus heard him say, "Go ye into all the world, preaching and teaching them all I have commanded you." In the following pages we glimpse the lives of three women God has called to do just as Christ said. These women have each lived out their ministry in the last quarter of the twentieth century in North America. Not unlike women of the gospel before them, they have had to overcome the biases of a society that was not fully open to their gender or color. They have been overcomers of the biases because of a persistent faith held firm by the Holy Spirit.

Myopic interpretations of selected Scriptures regarding women, rather than the whole of Scripture, has met them in the form of congregational committees charged with the responsibility of interviewing and choosing a pastor. Even the very structures of the institutional church have at times mitigated against the fulfillment of the call of God on their lives. When God calls a woman and she says, "Yes, I will," can others—male or female—say that she may not? Would this not be presumptuous? The denial of God's freedom to call anyone is truly an awesome question to ponder. What could be understood as ecclesiology becomes a study in theology, as we read their stories. For each of the women whose stories we now share, their theology is grounded in the word of God, "the only infallible rule of faith and practice."

A Pastor's Story

Ruth M. Smith

I once read that God writes straight with crooked lines. That phrase describes the work of God in my life. That is the story of my ministry. I received my B.S. degree from a Lutheran college, my M.S. degree from a Jesuit University. I spent two years in a Moravian Seminary and two years in Anderson University School of Theology. I received the Master of Divinity degree from the Church of God School of Theology. What a crooked path for God to take to prepare me for the ministry!

I worked during my college years in the office of a construction company, then for fifteen years I taught high school chemistry and did some counseling. All this experience, plus a lot of odd jobs here and there, combined to make the crooked path God used to mold me and shape me for the ministry waiting for me in the Kingdom.

When I ponder God's call on my life, I am truly amazed. How can one not believe in miracles when it has seemed that I have lived one. It all started at home with my parents. They were fine Christian people who took me to Sunday school and church and insisted on attendance at the Christian Endeavor meetings. In our little country church I asked God into my life a thousand times so I would not go to hell. God was a fire escape for me during my youth. When I went

102

to college, I gave up all the profession of religion. In the academic world, science became my god. I was planning to become a medical doctor. Pre-med studies took all of my time. Then into my life came love like I had not known it before. We planned to be married, but by my senior year, there were many doubts about the decision we were making. The major problem in my mind was that he was not a Christian. I found this thought to be very strange since I was no longer a Christian either. I had not given God any consideration for years, but the problem persisted and I finally broke the engagement.

Application deadline for medical school was passed, so I decided to work for a year, save my money, then attend medical school the following year. I accepted a position teaching chemistry at a high school. I had not had training or courses in educational methods, so I was granted a one-year temporary certificate. As the year progressed, I really began to enjoy my students and teaching. The school asked me to continue as a permanent teacher, so I took the steps necessary for teacher certification and continued teaching for fifteen years.

During the first three years of teaching, I was totally involved in my career. I lived my life as I wanted to live it, without God. I had everything to make me happy—a good job, money to pay my bills, a nice apartment, friends, and lots of leisure activities, but I was not happy. Everyone thought I was happy because I could wear a great mask, but behind the smile, I was miserable and becoming more so as days passed.

I began to search for the meaning of life. I already knew the answer was not in science, so I began to study philosophy. Every philosopher I read seemed to be a nihilist, and I concluded that there was no meaning in life. This lack of answers added to my dilemma.

Coinciding with my search was Earth Day, the day that was dedicated to the thrust of making people aware of pollution and the need to clean up the environment. As a science teacher, I was very much involved. All the implications of the problems of pollution on the peoples of the earth added to my already heavy heart. Here I was, not able to find meaning to my life, confronted with the fact that I was taking up valuable space on earth, drinking water and breathing air that other people would someday need. Other people obviously had meaning to their lives; everybody seemed to have found meaning; everybody but me.

My friends were happy, or at least they seemed happy. I decided to choose the friend who was the happiest, go to her, and ask her what her values were. My reasoning was that if I could find the right values and set priorities, then I could work toward realizing those values and find happiness and contentment. The values that I had did not seem to be worth living for. I asked my friend what made life worth living for her. She laughed at me. She said that she did not know what her values were, that she just lived life. She said that I was crazy and losing my mind. I agreed with my friend and my depression increased a hundredfold.

My search for meaning continued for more than a year and a half. My depression became deeper and deeper. Finally, one night sitting alone in my apartment, I made a decision. I went to the closet, got out my 357 Magnum pistol, loaded it, and decided to end it all. I was not afraid of pulling the trigger. I had done a lot of hunting, and killing me was going to be just like killing a deer.

I sat there with the pistol lying in my lap, thinking that surely someone could explain the meaning of life to me. I sat there wishing that I could find a truly wise person to help me find the meaning of life. Then, the thought entered my mind that Solomon had been the wisest man who ever lived. (I guess I had learned that in Sunday school.) I remember wishing with all my heart that he were alive and could talk to me. Then I remembered that Solomon had written the book of Ecclesiastes in the Bible.

Immediately I put the pistol down and went back into the closet to search for my old Bible from Sunday school. I knew that I had not thrown it away; it was in one of those unpacked boxes far back in the closet. I found the Bible, and I found Ecclesiates. I began to read.

Up to this point, none of my friends could understand my feelings, and their lack of understanding had made me feel that I was the only person ever who had not been able to find meaning to life. As I read that book in the Bible, I was amazed. I could not believe that Solomon was describing my feelings exactly. I felt joy in the common search for meaning. This wise man experienced the same feeling that I had experienced. My heart soared. I read every page rapaciously. I read to the end of the book, and his conclusion was God. My heart sank; this was no answer. I had begun with God. Was not God the one I had heard about all my childhood and teen-age years? Was not God the one I had accepted a thousand times so I would not go to hell?

Then the thought entered my mind: maybe the God of my childhood was just that, a child's God. Now that I was an adult, maybe there was more to God than I knew. Perhaps I should give this God another chance; perhaps I should give me another chance with God.

I continued this search through my thoughts, and finally came to a conclusion. I said to God, "Okay, God, I don't know if you even exist, but if you do, I want you to do everything that you can to make me aware of your existence. My part of this deal will be to do everything that I can to find you. I will give us both sixty days. If after sixty days, there is no change, then I will use the pistol and complete the job."

I got up from the chair, put the pistol away, went to the calendar, counted sixty days, and marked the sixtieth day with a big red X. I returned to the rocker and sat down again. I felt good about the deal. Then I began to question, What do I do now? How do I keep my side of the bargain. Then another thought came to me: God even works straight with all kinds of crooked thoughts! Jesus was supposed to be God. If I am to find God, perhaps I should research this Jesus.

Being the scientist that I was, I got my legal pad, my pencil, and the Bible, turned to the Gospels, and began to study this Jesus. I carefully read what he said, what he did, everything about Jesus that I could read in the Gospels. I was so absorbed in this study that every night after supper, I would get everything out and diligently search the Scriptures. It was an amazing study, and all my energies went into it. One day I looked at the calendar and saw the red X. I burst into laughter. My depression had not only disappeared, but I had no doubt that God existed, that God loved me so much that Jesus came to carry my sins and to die for my salvation. I had asked God into my life. God had come in and had brought the meaning for which I had searched so long. More than all that, God was beginning to transform me, Ruth, into a totally new person.

I say beginning, because as I look back on that crooked straight path, I see that God is still in the process of recreating me. God continued to use me in teaching and helping students; then I heard God calling me to become a pastor.

At first I could not believe that God was calling me. I was going through the deep grief experience of losing my best and closest friend to cancer. When I heard God's voice that day as I walked through my living room, I said, "Well, the grief has taken its toll; I am hearing things now." When God persisted, I responded that such could not be. I had been in seven different denominations and none of them allowed women to preach. These churches did not make much room for singles, and I was both female and single, anyway, I did not much like churches. Church people seemed to have an innate ability to hurt other people and I was not going to set myself up to be walked on and hurt.

I was walking with God on the crooked straight path. During my friend's bout with cancer, God had led us to a little church located on a back street a couple of blocks from our home. It was a Church of God congregation (Anderson, Indiana) and the pastor was a woman. The group was small, filled with old people, and did not have much of a program. This small church was different from other churches that I had attended. But there I was, and after going through the experience of grief, I did not have any energy for looking for another church. This small congregation had helped and the people were very kind to us during the difficult times. I decided to stay for a while, but I was not going to get involved. I would keep my mouth shut about any talents or abilities that I might have.

God said to me, "What if I ask you to help there? Would you?" I answered, "You know that I would do anything for you, God. If they ask me to do something, I will accept it as coming from you and I will try." A few weeks later, the pastor came to me and asked me to try to start a youth group. How God works! I had worked with youth groups in the other churches that I had attended.

That was just the beginning. All the theology that God had taught me in all those nights of studying my Bible was basically the theology of the Church of God. In 1976, when God called me to full-time ministry, I accepted my place in the fellowship of believers in the Church of God. Again, by a crooked straight path God was at work in my life.

It seems that I have always given God a hard time. When I was struggling with the issue of women in the ministry, I told God that I would go to the Moravian Seminary in Bethlehem, Pennsylvania, (near my home) to prove that I was not called to be a pastor. God showed me during the two years that I was in seminary that I was gifted to be a pastor. I finally accepted God's call to me, and with that reassurance of God at work in my life, I entered the School of Theology in Anderson, Indiana, to complete the Master of Divinity Degree.

In 1980, God called me to Glen Burnie, Maryland, to pastor a very, very small congregation. The Church of God does not seem to call women to large churches, so God calls us to small ones and does a large work there. When I arrived in Glen Burnie, I was told that there were thirty-five members; however, after some persons left the congregation because their new pastor was a woman, and other persons left because this was a good time to leave a dying congregation, there were eighteen people left in the congregation.

With these dedicated few, we decided to scrap the antiquated by-laws and to appoint boards and committees as they were needed to do the work of the congregation. I had never pastored before and I had thought that seminary had taught me how to pastor, but I found myself unsure of everything and praying for wisdom and guidance continually.

The words of my dad buoyed my spirits. Before accepting this pastorate, I had been struggling with the attitude this church held toward women as pastors. I was being offered this small church in Maryland that had no budget, and that needed the district organization to pay part of my salary. In effect this church was going to close down if something did not happen. My dad said to me, "Ruth, who do you think you are? You have never pastored before; you do not know how to pastor. You have everything to gain from Glen Burnie. If you get there and it does not succeed, nobody will blame you. Everyone will say that the church was in such sad condition that nobody could save it. But if you get there and learn and get the church going again, then you will gain everything—experience, wisdom, and you will have a church that is alive again. You cannot lose. Go for it."

We went for it—the new woman pastor, those eighteen people, and God. All of us put all we had into it. We prayed as we had never prayed before. We put our faith to the highest test. We took God's promises at face value. We learned to be honest with each other and with God. We learned to listen to each other and to God. We all learned and we all grew. The one who learned the most and grew the most had to be me, the new woman pastor. I thought that I knew God, but I grew to know God even better. I thought that I had faith, but I learned what faith really is. I thought I was a worker, but I learned what real work is.

We started a building fund, and after three years, God seemed to open some doors and to indicate to us that we should begin to draw plans for our new building. I had told God that I would walk through doors as they opened. After one and a half more years of planning, we began to build the new structure. We had $15,000 in our Building Fund, and now there were forty people. We needed an architect and there was no money for such an expensive service. We prayed and God supplied us with an architect who offered to work with us and to do the entire job for $5,500, including the surveying. There were more miracles as we subcontracted all the work out, took bids, and bought all the materials.

One of our fears was that we would get so far and run out of money. We decided to build in phases, completing one phase and having the money on hand before starting the next phase. The amazing aspect about this program was that when we completed phase one and paid the bills, we had enough money to proceed with phase two. That is the way the building was built from phase one to the final phase a year and a half later. We had paid out in cash $100,000. It was truly a miracle that God had worked with our prayers and our hard work. We celebrated with a Praise Service. Two years after we had begun the construction, we dedicated the new building worth more than a half million dollars. The congregation had grown to fifty-five members. In the years since the dedication, God has continued to work with us, and the congregation has continued to grow in numbers and in service.

After eight years of pastoring, I have concluded that:

> God does still work in great and mighty ways if we seek guidance in prayer and faith;
> God does call and work through women in the Church;
> God needs male and female, all working together in the harmony of the Spirit;
> And, my final conclusion is still that God writes straight with crooked lines.

A Preacher—Called of God

June D. Strickland

A great mystery in godliness is how and when the divine communicates with the human. The infinite relating to the finite stretches my mind at its most creative moment. My imagination explodes when I try to comprehend God speaking to me.

Between the ages of two and eight years, I lived in a rural home in southwestern Ohio with my parents, an older sister, and a younger sister. Our house stood on a hill, and late in the afternoons I often climbed the hill beyond our house to be alone and to talk to God. I was very young and cannot remember what I said to God, but I cannot forget that we communicated. God and I were on top of the world. From my vantage point on that hill, I could see the great Armco Steel Plant two miles away. Armco employed most of the area's working populous, yet it was a speck in God's hand. I recall with clarity a feeling of being in the presence of one who was bigger than anything or anyone. I was as sure then as I am now that there was nothing or no one anywhere that God did not understand; there was no one in whom God was not interested; there was no one that God could not or would not encircle with loving care. More importantly, in my tiny soul, I was sure that God knew me. Much later in life my memory of these years caused me to internalize these words of Jeremiah:

> "Before I formed you in the womb I knew you,
> before you were born I set you apart;
> I appointed you as a prophet."
> —Jeremiah 1:5 (NIV)

My parents made their commitment to Christ three years before I was born. I was raised in the church. I attended my first church service when I was two weeks old and have been in Sunday school and church regularly ever since. It is unusual that I cannot remember a Sunday school teacher that I had. I am sure that there were many dedicated and gifted teachers, but somehow my mind did not permanently register their names and faces.

Preaching is another story. I can recall the mannerisms, approximate age, body build, facial features, and expressions of many preachers. Not only did I listen to the preacher, I studied him or her as only a child can. While I was very young, I decided whether they were preaching out of burden or habit. Their level of effectiveness, in my mind, was equal to their level of conviction. I could not have articulated this, but I knew whether the preacher was prepared or was bluffing it. I detected expressions of ego, or the lack of them, long before I knew what ego meant. The preacher's degree of concern and compassion for those to whom he or she was preaching was always measured in my ears. I could feel, perhaps every child can, the response of the congregation to the message.

I love to hear the word proclaimed. Preaching is very separate from speaking. The preacher can speak, but a speaker cannot preach unless she or he is called of God. I have the deepest respect for God's call to the preacher.

In my early teens the devil bid very high for my affection and allegiance. Those destructive years were a time of need in my life. I had many friends in high school, among them one committed Christian. She was very sensitive to my spiritual needs and let me know that she was praying for me.

On a Sunday evening, in my home church, we were having a youth emphasis service. I was in the choir with most of the other youth. I had not stopped attending church, but I had stopped listening. The speaker for this special service was hard to ignore even by a rebellious teenager. He stood up to preach and my childhood ability to critique returned. Before he had finished his first sentence I had decided he was called of God and had something to say to me that night. He preached on hell, and his heart was broken. It was not my fear of hell as much as his broken heart that determined my giving my life unstintingly to God.

In response to the Word preached, the work of Christ and the invitation of the Spirit, I was saved. From that moment I wanted to please God. I said in every prayer, "God, I will do anything you want me to do." I meant it, but I did not know it would mean preaching. Even with the fascination I had always had with preaching, I never suspected that I would be a preacher. There was not a preacher on either side of my family tree, but at sixteen years of age I knew, deep in my heart, God was calling me to preach.

During the following three years, God and I had an ongoing debate. Obviously the issue of a woman preacher had to be addressed, at least for me. With God it must not matter since Paul proclaimed to the Galatians, "In Christ we are neither male nor female" (3:28). A servant is a servant. Paul had it settled, but for me it was a daily struggle. My mind traveled again and again to the women I had heard preach.

I remembered a very young evangelist who, in her teens, preached powerfully. I remembered a lovely middle-aged woman evangelist who had eaten dinner in our home when I was probably five years old. I recalled an older woman pastor who proclaimed God's truth with tremendous conviction and confidence. Vividly I recalled her preaching when my vocally expressive Pastor Clifford Hutchinson said aloud, "That is the truth!" She stopped her message, looked him squarely in the eyes and stated clearly, "I do not preach anything but the truth." I was impressed! The audience laughed, but I computed a preaching rule: If it is not truth, it is not preaching. Another woman, probably in her late twenties, spoke directly to my heart the one time that I heard her preach. I would often think of Lillie McCutcheon—so prepared, so intelligent, so articulate, so single-minded, so deep, so used of God and accepted by the Church. Each of these women left me with a good impression. Role models they were. But there was one woman whose brash manner and self-serving attitude was quite offensive. She had a leading role as I prepared my case against God. I definitely did not want—and God knew I did not want—any identity with a self-centered preacher, male or female. Besides, my heartcry was with Jeremiah: "Ah, Sovereign God, . . . I do not know how to speak; I am only a child" (Jeremiah 1:6, NIV).

In those three years I did not talk to anyone about the call I felt I had. It had been completely between God and me. I argued with God for months and months. I even "fell in love" with a minister and bargained with God: I will marry him and he can preach. That seemed like a good idea at the time, however, the minister married someone else, and still I was called to preach and I knew it.

At nineteen, after one semester in college, I surrendered my life to preach God's word. I had not wrestled with God for three years in vain. After dealing with the Almighty I came clean with this commitment:

All I am,
All I am not,
All I ever hope to be
is yours, God.
I accept your call and will
be faithful to that call
regardless of the cost.

There has been a price to pay. At times, it has seemed high, but never has the cost been worthy of being compared with the honor of being called by God. Preaching is divine and can only be justified with a divine call.

In preaching, God pursues, we submit; God calls, we respond; God imparts, we accept. For the preacher-to-be, I would paraphrase Matthew 6:33: But accept ye first your call to preach and all these other things will be added to you.

In May 1966, I, June Downing Middlebrooks, graduated from Gulf Coast Bible College in Houston, Texas, with a Bachelor of Theology degree. Immediately after graduation I moved to Freeport, Texas, to join my husband who was already there as assistant manager of the Kroger Supermarket. In August our first daughter, Aaren Rene' was born. By the time Aaren was a toddler my husband had been transferred to the Kroger store in Galveston, Texas. Our home was in Texas City, twenty-five miles from Galveston where I became assistant to Senior Pastor Edwin C. Ogle at the First Church of God. In this church I received two years of apprentice training and experience in preaching and pastoral care.

In January 1969, when I was twenty-five years old, the First Church of God in Atlanta, Texas, called me to serve as pastor of their congregation. My husband was employed at that time by the Safeway store in Atlanta.

In November of 1970 I joined the staff at First Church of God in Dallas, Texas, as associate pastor. James H. Curtis was the senior pastor. In moving to Dallas we were returning to my husband's hometown. He continued to work for Safeway, and he served as youth co-ordinator at First Church of God.

In December 1972, our second child was born. Six weeks before the birth of the baby, my husband of ten years left me, his family, and the church. I was numb. I was bewildered. There were moments of anger, questions of guilt, feelings of helplessness, moments of utter loneliness, hours before God asking for answers and strength to meet the needs of each day. Gradually God's reassuring answers came through the promises of the Word. I took a month's leave from the church, and one week before Christmas a beautiful baby girl was born. Amy Richelle was pure joy to her older sister and to me. The responsibility of her care kept my tormented mind and broken heart in some semblance of normalcy. The church was very gracious to me during that traumatic holiday season, and gave me many expressions of love and care.

In January 1973, my husband filed for divorce and in April the divorce was final. My marriage was ended. I was a divorced woman. Would the church still accept me as minister and pastor? I badly needed an affirmation from the church. I requested a vote of confidence. The vote was taken, and a large majority supported my ministry. The few who did not support my ministry added to my pain and self-doubt. Seven months later I resigned and started working in a bank in downtown Dallas.

After three months at the bank, I decided to go home to my mom and dad in Ohio. My spirit was broken and my future looked very bleak. I knew that I was called of God, but that is all I knew. I was in Ohio three months without a trace of hope for employment of any kind.

At the same time in a small cotton farming community out in West Texas a few precious people had lost their beloved pastor. I had been with the congregation in a revival in 1970. Juanita Hester, the pulpit committee chair, called me in Ohio and asked if I would come to serve as their pastor for the summer. She said that after the summer the church would make decisions about the future ministry of the church. I went with my two little girls, by then Amy was eighteen months and Aaren was eight years old, to live in a furnished mobile home in Ira, Texas. Eventually it was amusing to us all, but their initial concern was that I was a woman pastor and that I was divorced.

Healing came in the hot, dry climate of West Texas and the people and pastor flourished. I served this congregation for eleven years, including fourteen months in Clovis, New Mexico. During this ministry, two lovely buildings were added to the church property, attendance tripled, and the annual budget increased 800 percent. For several years the church has distinguished itself as a challenge church in World Service giving. The Women of the Church of God unit, formed in 1978, had a budget in 1985 larger than our entire church budget had been in 1974.

In May 1981, I married Elbert Strickland. Both of us have suffered significant losses, which added to our conviction that God brought us together. We are presently serving in East Texas. Elbert sold his welding service of twenty-nine years to make the move to Nacogdoches, Texas, where I am senior pastor of the First Church of God. I believe every experience of my life has brought me safely to this place for this time.

After twenty-six years of preaching and eighteen years as pastor, this is my summary: We dare not offer God anything but our very best. We insult a great God if we do not ask and expect great things. I have never been happier to be a preacher, called and used of God.

Church Planter

Vivian G. Moore

Vivian Moore, church planter, still sounds strange to me. It was not on my original agenda, but as I turned my life completely over to God, church planting became one of the agenda items for my life. God can and does use anyone male or female, black or yellow or white, young or old, to accomplish the work of the church.

In the mid 1930s, my father the late Reverend James C. Radden became a "come-outer." I am told that from his earliest existence he had always possessed an unusual inquisitiveness about God, salvation, and the hereafter. I was told that his sense of values and morals was always above reproach. He always felt comfortable and looked forward to attending church with his family. His father, Thomas Radden, was a deacon in the Baptist church they attended.

Upon leaving South Carolina and going to Virginia at about the age of seventeen, my father continued his quest for knowledge about God and answers to his many questions. In Richmond, Virginia, he was introduced to a small band of "holiness" people. He soon discovered that this little band led by Reverend Willie Curry was part of a group known as the Church of God. The Holy Spirit quickly let my father know that his inner yearning and search was over. My father had found God's people. He often referred to the experience as "finding the truth, and coming into the light."

He later met and married my mother, Beatrice Winston, a talented, artistic teacher, and together they worshiped at the Church of God. They experienced many obstacles as they tried to help their family understand this new religion. At that time teachings about the Holy Spirit, the unity of all believers, and sanctification were virtually new doctrines. Dad boldly proclaimed his faith, studied the Word, worked in the church as a teacher, Sunday school superintendent, deacon, and finally a pastor.

In February 1941, I was born into that loving Christian home. Now my parents were the proud parents of two daughters, Delores Anita and me, Vivian. Shortly after I was born, my mother realized that her two special children would be used of God. She was also aware that because of illness that she would not live to care for us. She began to talk to my father about her sense of God's call for her and her concern for us. Later she contracted spinal meningitis and a cure was not to be taken for granted during those years. Facing this new awareness she asked three major things of my father—upon her deathbed—he must stay with God, keep all of us together as a family, and last he must educate us. In my eighteenth month my mother went to be with the Lord. I have no memory of this, but my sister Delores vividly recalls the happening.

At only twenty-five years of age my father was left a widower with two young daughters. He stayed with God, with the Church of God, and kept the family together. Several years later, he was married to my stepmother Juanita Spruell. Together they worked to provide a Christian home for us.

My childhood memories are of a strong committed Christian home with a distinct code of ethics. Our entire lives revolved around the church. My parents through example showed and taught us about loving the Lord and the church. I am told that at the age of three I asked my dad if I could be baptized. I wanted to be saved. So at the age of three I was baptized in the Saint James River in Richmond, Virginia. I was encouraged at a young age to actively participate in church activities. We were in later years taught to assume the responsibility of leadership. Dad always emphasized that the pastor's family must lead the way in loving, caring, serving, and giving. I must admit, I did not always like the required commitment that was expected, but nevertheless I always complied.

In the 1950s our family moved to Chicago, Illinois, after a year and a half stay in Greenville, South Carolina. In Chicago we began attending the Langley Avenue Church of God pastored by the late Reverend S.P. Dunn. At the Langley Avenue church, under the very able teachings of Pastor Dunn, I became a student of the Word. I experienced a spirit-filled, dynamic church in operation. He was a brilliant teacher and a master administrator and pulpiteer. People now are attempting to develop cell ministries, undershepherd ministries, evangelistic Bible study groups—Pastor Dunn had these ministries already in place in the 1950s. Some of his teachings were noninclusive and thus prevented the unification of the many Church of God congregations. Consequently, as a child I never enjoyed the fellowship of some of the now leading congregations in the Chicago area. Pastor Dunn's support of the annual Anderson International

Convention led me to make it a yearly experience. My life was greatly influenced by the ministries of the Langley Avenue fellowship.

The church that my father pastored for more than thirty years became a church after having been one of the "districts" of the Langley Avenue Church outreach ministry. The city and metropolitan area were divided into districts each having its own minister. The fellowship groups met weekly in their respective area and then came to the Langley Avenue Church on Sunday. This district ministry is comparable to that of Reverend Cho's outreach ministry in Korea.

District twenty-six was assigned to my father. This was my first major introduction to church planting. We began having a Tuesday evening Bible study in Chicago Heights. I vividly remember the telephone calls, the collecting of Bibles, chairs, hymn books, the car pools, the extra guests at our dinner table, and the sacrificial giving.

At first it was difficult to understand why my father would choose to leave a large, beautiful church to work with a handful of people. My father always chose to work and worship in small struggling congregations, to affiliate with and identify with their challenge. I was disappointed when we left the Langley Avenue church family since I had always anticipated being in Sister Vera Pitts Morris's young adult choir. One of the rules was that one had to be age sixteen. As soon as I became old enough, after waiting all those years, my father's new mission took us away. At the new mission there would be no established choir, youth ministry, music program, effective Sunday school, not even a maintenance staff. At first we even shared facilities with another church. There were not enough chairs; we used couches for pews.

The next move was to a storefront. My sister and I were expected to perform janitorial duties regularly in preparation for the Sunday services. Throughout these experiences our family's financial support constituted nearly three-fourths of the church's budget. Again, I did not realize that many years hence I would use this valuable training. I am glad that I was taught to give cheerfully. I was taught that tithing was not an option. If the church needed anything and it was within our power we were taught to give. We were taught that leadership must set the example in giving of finances, time and talent. We were also taught that when we gave, we gave without expecting to receive honor and glory on earth.

Little did I know that I was in training for my future vocation. My sister and I sang, led devotions, gave inspirational talks, taught Sunday school, ushered, developed curriculum, canvassed from house to house to evangelize the nonchurched, and visited the sick. We never expected committees to be assigned to do those tasks. We were the preacher's kids and we simply thought that we were supposed to serve wherever and whenever needed.

Today I am often amused at the controversy of women being active in the church. As far back as I can remember we were taught that we were special, gifted children, and that God expected more from us. Sexism was never a part of my upbringing. I was unaware that I was supposed to be "quiet," to stay in the background, not to have opinions, thoughts, and so forth. We were always allowed to discuss and to share our opinions. We were constantly encouraged to read. Our example was seeing my father read profusely. Relative to division of responsibility, we were taught that we were to work in our area of competence, and that was not gender related. Hence, my role as a church planter is really not as a novice. I believe that my whole life has been preparing me for this task.

I attended elementary school and high school in Chicago Heights, Illinois. I graduated from Anderson University in June of 1962. One of the major highlights in my father's life was for his daughter to attend college in Anderson. He loved Anderson, Indiana, the headquarters of our church. After graduation I was prepared to teach secondary education.

Those early years were times of change, turmoil, discovery, awakening, growth, and much disappointment. Leaving Anderson University to return home, back into the old environment was quite an adjustment. The church and its people seemed different. I realized that the people at home were different from the church and the people at school. I often felt like an outsider. I questioned many practices and traditions. The knowledge that I had spent four years acquiring was not always understood and accepted. I really did feel like a woman without a country.

There was a ray of hope. I had the opportunity to visit a church pastored by Reverend Williams on the south side of Chicago. The pastor and people seemed to have beliefs and values similiar to mine. I soon learned, however, that this church was in transition. The neighborhood had changed and the church was planning to move to another location. I have always had difficulty comprehending why a church must move when the neighborhood's composition changes.

After teaching for several years, I was married in 1965. In 1968 we were blessed with a beautiful daughter, Evelyn Bernice, affectionately referred to as Evie. Very soon after Evie was born our family moved to St. Louis, Missouri.

The next few years were years of great change, growth, disappointment, renewal, new friends, and finally healing. As the years passed, God provided many new experiences. I was the recipient of a Fellowship to Washington University to work on a Masters degree and an advanced graduate degree in Administration. I received numerous awards, honors, and opportunities for advancement and recognition. The Lord was preparing me for my ministry by developing my organizational and administrative skills. It seemed that my life was not to be that of an uninvolved spectator. Professionally, I was often expected to "walk on water," and always it seemed I was representing my race. I have often felt that I have not had a normal existence because it was always expected that I would assume leadership to effect change.

Early in the seventies I had the opportunity to help start another church. The community did not have a black church, although it had a strong Jewish and Christian heritage. Initially the church began in a storefront. We were able to turn a simple place into a beautiful chapel. Later, I spoke to a local Presbyterian church about allowing us to use their chapel. The pastor of that congregation asked his Board, and history was made. The St. Louis Post Dispatch wrote a feature story about the two churches. As I look back on that experience I now realize that what we accomplished without a board, budget, or task force was to get a church established. That church now has a membership of over one thousand.

Even then we were using bona fide church planting techniques without having the benefit of how to do it workshops. Many of our early members were the result of person-to-person evangelism. Some of these members were students from my classes, neighbors, and sometimes next door neighbors. Our present pastor and his wife were a part of that nucleus. That was nearly twenty years ago. I never dreamed that one day the Parhams would pastor a newly planted Community Church of God in North St. Louis county. These were exciting times! We were able to touch so many lives. We used everything we had to help establish the new church. Much of life serves as a preparation period for something better to come.

In the 1970s I began worshiping with the First Church of God in St. Louis. Reverend Arlo Newell was the pastor and during my difficult times he was my counselor. When he left St. Louis, Reverend Emmitt Whalen became the new pastor. He patiently counseled and prayed with me as I went through my Gethsemane. At the time, these pastors were the only ministers other than my father to whom I could bare my soul. To everyone else I projected professionalism, sophistication, utter confidence, and the picture of success. Little did they realize the turmoil that simmered inside of me.

In 1976 when I was named "Teacher of the Year," Reverend Whalen made contact with Anderson University and subsequently, I received a call from Dr. Reardon who was then president of Anderson University offering me a position in the University. After much prayer and consultation with my father, we felt that God wanted me to stay in the St. Louis area, to complete graduate school and to wait for further direction from God. I now know that God's will was for me to help establish another church.

After Reverend Whalen left First Church of God in St. Louis, Reverend Andrew Bugg became the new pastor. Reverend Bugg became my pastor, friend, mentor, and my real source of encouragement and support. He shared my dream. We both believed that it was possible to have a vibrant, progressive, spirit-filled integrated congregation in St. Louis. Pastor Bugg made a concerted effort to involve himself in the black community. He met with and fellowshiped with some of the leading black community and religious leaders. He strongly stood by his conviction that all of God's people should worship together. He ministered to black families by meeting them at their point of need and reinforced the message that Christ died for all. Of course Pastor Bugg's dreams were not shared or fully understood by all. After several years of untiring work he went on to another area of ministry.

Throughout the years there had been dialogue about First Church of God moving to another location. Always in the back of my mind I wondered what would happen if that ever occurred. It seemed that I always had a restlessness in my spirit as the topic was discussed.

The 1980s brought a new direction for my life. Professionally I was an assistant principal at a predominantly white high school. I was referred to locally and nationally as a community leader. My spiritual life was growing and developing at a rapid pace. To most people it would appear that I had the world in my hand. However, I knew that something was missing. I was being made to finally address God's call in my life to the ministry in the church. I could no longer ignore the call. For years I had put my ministry under a different label. Under the spiritual leadership of Reverend Curtis Barge, I finally accepted my call and all of the implications and new directions that would ensue.

Making that decision was one of the most difficult decisions that I have ever had to make. I did not feel that I should be the one God wanted. I did not look the part; I did not feel the part. I could not understand why I could not continue doing what I was doing under the old label. I was known as being very religious. I really did not like the changes that I felt that I would have to make. I was only six hours away from a doctoral degree in Educational Adminis- tration at Washington University, and now I would have to systematically start a theological course of training. Finally, after much soul searching and negotiation, I decided that if this must be, so let it be. But I did not want people to call me Reverend Moore. I decided that Sister Moore or Vivian was quite sufficient.

I found the credentials process one that was stimulating and enriching. A prolific reader, I began the newest aspect of my pilgrimage of faith. Earlier it seemed that God had turned my reading interest to church growth and new churches. I began to read the newest literature in that area. I attended local seminars on church growth. However, it was in a church business meeting that a brother's statement punctured my spirit. Here I was again in a setting where the neighborhood was changing. People felt that there was a shortage of potential growth and they felt it was time to look for a new location. Here was an area that was going to provide new opportunities for evangelism. The result would be a coming together of God's people. From that moment, I decided that we had to work where the need was and to stop running. In my own experience many of my professional colleagues had asked me where I worshiped. In my heart I knew that many of them having been raised in the black experience would not enjoy a service where the black experi- ence was totally absent. God let me know that I was to help establish a vibrant, spirit-filled, Bible teaching fellowship that would embrace God's love for all people including black professionals.

After much prayer and deliberation, I decided to discuss the matter with my husband, Frank Moore. He was on the board of trustees at the First Church of God, deeply involved with the church and had never discussed the possiblity of worshiping elsewhere. To my amazement, he shared my vision of a new congregation. He immediately began making suggestions and implementing plans. His enthusiasm was contagious. Subsequently, I discussed my vision with Reverend Barge. At the time he was hospitalized, but he immediately felt that God was leading and he willingly offered his support. A short time later I made contact with Reverend Pearlie Anderson. I began telling her about the new church vision. She was anxious to lend support to this challenging endeavor. Thus, the nucleus began to take form. We began having informal meetings to discuss our plans for church planting. I wrote letters of intent to Reverend Ivory Bailey, Jr., chair of the local ministerial assembly, to Reverend Lloyd Bowen, state coordinator, and to Reverend Ken Vanderlaan, church planting coordinator. We immediately received moral support and encouragement for the new church.

In November 1986, we had our first public Bible study. It was held at the Northside Christian Church. Nearly thirty people came for our study on the Abundant Life. We shared a rich fellowship following the Bible study. Each member of our nucleus group had sent personal invitations to family and friends announcing the formation of our group. It is difficult to describe the excitement and anticipation we felt as we handed the name tags and study outlines to the people as they arrived. We could feel God sanctioning our efforts.

Fortunately, within two weeks of our initial Bible study, I was able to attend a Church Planting Seminar at Fuller Seminary in California. Those November days in California were ones that made an indelible impression in my life. There were hundreds of people from all over the world representing more than thirty denominations, gathered to learn how to plant a church. As the various groups were announced, those of us from the Church of God, Anderson, Indiana, immediately gravitated to each other and found a common bond. While in California, God began to show me how the Community Church of God in North St. Louis County would evolve.

The winter of 1986 was significant to the new group. Many of the members began feeling a need for a Sunday worship experience. We began exploring the possiblities. We had previously been looking for a place for public worship but now the need was urgent. As I reflect now upon the situation I realize that this was a time when we should have prayed for more direction. I believe that we should have developed a cohesive and strong nucleus before we began our public worship experience. Although I am told continuously that we are doing so well, I do not want the Community Church to be another small, struggling fellowship. From the beginning God has made it known to me that the new church must be a vital vibrant, spirit-filled, Bible-centered fellowship. I knew that it would be nontraditional but that would be its strong point.

Our first public worship service was held on Easter Sunday, 1987. It was truly a time of celebration. More than seventy people gathered for this service. Reverend Curtis Barge was the speaker. In preparation for this service, seven thousand letters were mailed to the surrounding communities inviting them to worship with us. Each member of the nucleus was assigned a specific task. We prayed daily for this service that God would be the center of this worship experience. A praise team had been developed to provide the music for the day. Since no musician was a part of the nucleus, we hired an organist. All of the members and friends shared in a fellowship hour at the close of the service.

The first six months of our fellowship represented a time of growth, introspection, reevaluation, and a continual focus on defining what God had ordained for us to do. The summer of 1987 was a long, hard summer. We lost some of the leadership support, our finances were low, our attendance sporadic.

I shall never forget my return from the Church of God International Conference in Korea. I was met with some unpaid bills and a noticeable reduction of Wednesday evening participants. As I paid the musicians I remembered the commitment that I had made. My finances were given to me by God. All that I had belonged to God, therefore I must give it back to God. God had and still has much work to do with me in some areas in that regard. I have had difficulty understanding how people can know the financial situation of a fellowship and yet expect to be paid for everything that they do. This was and is an area that I have had to leave in God's hands. I have given more hours than many full-time or bi-vocational pastors without gratuity, but kingdom building is not measured by hours, salary packages, or promotional opportunities. I thank God daily for heavenly love and care and for the bountiful blessings bestowed upon us. It is our intent to continue to give, serve, and support the church until God directs us otherwise.

After the long summer of 1987, I felt that God wanted us to have a strong senior pastor. As our group began to pray about this new direction we sought counsel from our state and national leaders. Several persons were suggested as possible candidates. In January 1988, Reverend Dale Schaffler came to serve as our pastor. He was a retired pastor from Michigan. With God's help he had worked with a small church that was thought to be dying. God used him to help revitalize that congregation and now it is a vibrant congregation with a new facility and a new vision. Pastor Schaffler remained with us through the spring. We found ourselves again without senior pastoral leadership.

We were approached by another denomination to merge with them. Interestingly, although that group was a newly planted one, it had full financial support from their national body. However, the group had not grown and was struggling for existence. They were excited about our fellowship and felt that the two groups could effectively co-exist and minister together.

The Community church felt that God wanted us to exist as part of the Church of God movement. We believed that our message of love, unity, holiness, and wholeness was one that the community needed. Even though a merger would have meant full financial support including a facility and a seminary trained pastor, we believed that we could not compromise. Again we began to pray for a leader who would be our pastor. We knew that God had someone for us.

Mother's Day was about six weeks away. Traditionally, in many black congregations a woman speaks on Mother's Day. As I began to pray about our possibilities one name kept recurring. I could not understand this, since the person was already a member of a very large church where her entire family was involved. Finally, I decided to call the person, Agnes Parham. She immediately said, "I can't speak." I related to her that I believed that God had indeed put her name on my heart. Then she asked me to talk to her husband Doug. We talked and I told him a little about our church and why I had initially called Agnes. The Parhams had been a part of my earlier church planting experience. We had fellowshiped many times with this family, but had not thought our paths would cross again.

Mother's Day 1988 was the beginning of a new era in the life of Community Church of God. As the Parham family walked in the door we felt that they most certainly were going to feel led to be a part of our new church family. Previous to his coming, I had felt the need to share with him everything about this fellowship from its beginnings to the present. Our people immediately loved the Parham family. He was invited to speak on the Sunday following Mother's Day. He has spoken at every Sunday service since that time.

As time passed our people felt that we finally had our senior pastor. All the members shared this feeling. We felt that consensus was ratified by God. In July 1988, Community Church of God elected Douglas Parham as pastor. He had previously met with Pastor J.M. Taylor of First Church of God and with the state leaders. He believed that their move to the Church of God was a part of his pilgrimage of faith. He had been restless for a year at the previous church. He had resigned from all of the boards and was waiting to hear from God. Now he knows that God was getting him ready for this new phase in his life. Community Church of God has grown numerically as well as spiritually under his very able leadership. His love, faith, and commitment has been an inspiration to all of us.

There have been many joys, heartaches, sacrifices, and struggles through the years of church planting, but church planting is of God. It is a task that must be done. It cannot be done without God's hand of approval. It is not a task for the faint of heart or the easily discouraged or noncommitted. One has to say, I will go even if it means that I must make the journey alone. One has to be willing to give all to the cause and expect nothing but God's love and approval in return. One has to be willing not to be understood by other colleagues and friends. Yet, if God lays the burden of responsibility on your heart, you must go.

Vivian Moore, church planter, educator, civic leader, mother, wife, and child of God. I do not know what the future holds or where I will be. I do know who holds the future, and as I go I will go with God. "To God be the glory."

Cheryl Sanders

Cheryl Sanders is an ordained minister of the Church of God and is currently serving as Associate Pastor of Leadership Development at Third Street Church of God, in Washington, D.C. with Pastor Samuel G. Hines. She served as pastor of First Church of God in Boston, Massachusetts; as campus minister to black students at Harvard-Radcliffe; and as a chaplaincy intern in the Washington Hospital Center, Washington, D.C.

Sanders is Assistant Professor of Christian Ethics at Howard University Divinity School, Washington, D.C. Her B.A. degree in Mathematics and Black Studies is from Swarthmore College. She holds the Master of Divinity degree cum laude *and the Doctor of Theology degree from Harvard Divinity School in Applied Theology. She has received the Benjamin E. Mays Fellowship and the American Bible Society Prize.*

Her writings appear in several professional journals. "The Woman as Preacher" appeared in the 1986 Spring-Summer edition of the Journal of Religious Thought. *She was selected to participate in the Institute of Ecumenics in Bossey, Switzerland, where she led a group on "Teaching the Bible in Ecumenical perspective."*

Her ministry at Third Street Church of God includes responsibilities in staff development, lay leadership training, and supervision of seminarians interning in urban ministry. She is a professor and seminar leader in Afro-American Ethos and Ethic, Biblical Ethics, Contemporary Issues and Christian Social Ethics, Feminist Ethics, and Theology.

Chapter 8:

Ethics of Holiness and Unity in the Church of God

Cheryl Sanders

Ethics as a field of study is the analysis of human actions, institutions, and character using norms such as good and evil, right and wrong. Christian ethics evaluates these factors in light of Christian belief. Two characteristic themes of the Church of God reformation movement—holiness and unity—inform our ethics and shape our specific witness to the world as Christians. In this chapter we will examine Christian ethics in the doctrines of holiness and unity and explore the impact of sex and race upon the preaching and practice of ethics in the Church of God.

The Gospel of John records that prior to his arrest and crucifixion Jesus prayed for his disciples. The following excerpt from John 17 reveals Jesus' desire that his followers be sanctified and unified:

> Sanctify them by the truth; your word is truth. As you sent me into the world, I have sent them into the world. For them I sanctify myself, that they too may be truly sanctified. My prayer is not for them alone. I pray also for those who will believe in me through

their message, that all of them may be one, Father,
just as you are in me and I am in you. (John 17:17-
21, NIV)

The followers of Christ are sanctified or set apart for
sacred use by means of the word of God. In effect, it is by
heeding and adhering to divine truth as revealed in the Bible
that the Christian becomes fit to be used by God. The
purpose of sanctification is to qualify believers to be used by
God to present a message to the world that will enable
others to believe in Christ. Moreover, Jesus' prayer for the
unity of the believers signifies his understanding that unity is
necessary to establish the credibility of this witness to the
world. Thus sanctification and unity are key elements of
Jesus' prayer and God's plan for the mission of the church,
i.e., to be sent into the world as witnesses of divine truth.

A functional understanding of holiness and unity also
undergirds Paul's application of the (Old Testament) scriptures to the life of the church at Corinth. In his second
letter, Paul counsels the Corinthian believers to "come out"
and come together as one family under God:

"Therefore come out from them and be separate,
says the Lord. Touch no unclean thing, and I will
receive you." "I will be a Father to you, and you will
be my sons and daughters, says the Lord Almighty."
Since we have these promises, dear friends, let us
purify ourselves from everything that contaminates
body and spirit, perfecting holiness out of reverence
for God. (2 Cor. 6:17—7:1, NIV)

This exhortation to holiness and unity is couched in the
language of covenant and promise; the believers are set
apart to enter into covenant relationship as sons and daughters of God, and a practical response to receiving the promises of God is the pursuit of holiness as an act of worship.
The text also indicates that sanctification has two irreducible
dimensions—social and personal. The social dimension man-
dates separation from (i.e., "do not be yoked together with")
unbelievers on the one hand, and unification with believers

(i.e., with those who are the temple, people, children of God) on the other. The personal dimension requires each individual to guard against contamination of body and spirit.

These and other biblical texts form a firm foundation for the promotion of holiness and unity by the Church of God. The underlying theological assumptions and practical ethical implications of these doctrines are particularly illuminating with respect to the experience of women and minorities within the Church of God Reformation Movement.

Some Theological Assumptions Concerning the Attributes of God

The holiness and unity tradition in the Church of God derives its importance primarily from a biblical understanding of who God is and what God is like. Although a careful reading of scripture would reveal numerous characteristics of God, seven attributes have been selected for discussion here because they have a direct bearing upon the ethical imperative to holiness and unity. They are: (1) creativity; (2) love; (3) truth; (4) righteousness; (5) mercy; (6) grace and (7) holiness.

The first book of the Bible begins with an account of how the world came into being, and identifies God as Creator. Although the creation story is told in at least three different ways in the early chapters of Genesis (see chs. 1:1—2:3; 2:4-25; 5:1-2), each time the story is told the point is established that God created human beings in God's own image as male and female. Thus the world and those who inhabit it have one common origin as the handiwork of one Creator, who stamped an express self-image on humankind. It is implied that both the male and female bear the image of God, and no implication of inferiority or superiority among persons is implied in any of the three accounts. Even in the story of Adam and Eve, the woman is fashioned to be the man's partner or helper, again with no suggestion of subordination in role or function.

The most obvious reason for sexual differentiation, however, is for the purpose of procreation. Sexual difference is not established as a basis for discrimination or exploitation, but rather for the coming together of men and women to be fruitful in reproduction and to complement and support each other as responsible stewards of God's created order. Thus the union that occurs when a man and woman come together in the marriage relationship replicates the oneness of the Creator whose image is borne by the two. Moreover, the mutual attraction that occurs between the sexes generally is God's design to ensure that the human species will continue to reproduce its own kind. It should be noted that the concept of race as understood today is meaningless in the context of creation. God created one human race. Although there are different nationalities and languages and even colors of skin among the peoples of the Bible, clearly the notion of classifying human beings into separate groups called races based upon physical traits is an invention of modern anthropology serving the purposes of the ideology and politics of racism. The creation accounts never suggest that God intended for human beings to use their points of difference, sexual or otherwise, as a justification for hatred, but rather for unity and fruitfulness and partnership to God's glory.

God is love. If we define love as active concern for the well-being of others, then we can view the Bible in both Testaments as a history of God's expression of active concern for the well-being of the human family God created. The love of God is manifest in the many roles that God assumes in relation to persons: as Father, as Savior and Deliverer, and as comforting Spirit. The special appeal of John 3:16, the one biblical text that is perhaps memorized by more Christians than any other, is attributable to the fact that it simplifies and summarizes the good news of the gospel of Jesus Christ in terms of God's love for the world; "For God so loved the world, that he gave his only begotten Son, that whosoever believeth in him should not perish, but have everlasting life" (KJV). That love is God's fundamental motive in word and in action is apparent in this verse. It certainly provides the rationale for the concept of covenant, that is, the agreement of promise and protection that God repeatedly offers to Israel in the Old Testament and to Jew and Gentile alike in the New Testament. Our apprehension of God's love makes feasible our worship, our prayers, and our confessions, because our belief in a loving God becomes our assurance of finding the acceptance and help that we need. God's love extends to every creature, without regard to sex or race, yet if God shows any favoritism at all it is toward those whose need is greatest and who feel most urgently the desire for God's active concern. It is impossible to earn or demand God's love on the basis of merit; by the same token it is absurd to assume that only certain persons or groups are deserving of God's active concern.

Truth is an important attribute of God because God is the source of all truth, and God's word is true. The truth of God is fully demonstrated in God's trustworthiness; God can be trusted to perform everything that God has promised. The word of God, conveyed through the Bible, interpreted by faithful preachers and teachers, and tested and tried in the life of the believer, reflects the reality and reliability of God. Truth serves as the basis for discerning the purposes of God in human affairs as opposed to the false designs of the adversary. The Bible introduces the concept of evil in the book of Genesis; in the encounter between the serpent and the woman, evil is clearly identified with deceit and denial of the truth. In particular, this story illustrates how the fall of humankind into the misery of broken relationships with each other and with God begins with the denial of the truth. Relationships between individuals and groups suffer in the absence of truth, and truth-telling is a necessary foundation of human civilization and of human relationships of all kinds. To say that God is a God of truth is to acknowledge that we cannot fully hear or respond to God until we are willing to be absolutely truthful in God's presence.

Righteousness, simply stated, is the predisposition toward making things right. In the Bible righteousness is practically synonymous with justice, especially in relation to God, who is the source of righteousness and the ultimate Judge. Indeed God establishes and exemplifies the divine norms by which words and deeds and individuals and nations are judged.

Righteousness as justice includes such basic notions as fairness and equity. In divine perspective it implies doing all that is required to uphold what is right—teaching, testing, chastising, avenging, forgiving, restoring. In this regard both God's wrath and God's love are means by which righteousness is instituted and justice is served. God's righteousness is the ground of our justification, and the terms of the covenant God has devised for us require us to deal righteously and justly with our neighbor. This stipulation has special significance with reference to the poor and the disadvantaged; to withhold justice from the victims of oppression is to pour contempt upon the belief that God is the most righteous judge who exercises ultimate moral authority over all without regard to social or economic status.

In essence, mercy is gratuitous compassion. It is care expressed without regard to claims or rights. As an attribute of God, mercy complements righteousness without supplanting it. If justice rests upon the application of norms and standards and the imposition of penalties and rewards, mercy represents God's insistence that all are worthy of compassion, regardless of whatever else may be deserved or merited. An important element of the concept of mercy is the assumption that God occupies a superior vantage point, morally and otherwise, with respect to humankind, which in the eternal scheme of affairs gives God sole possession of the power and authority not only to judge, but also to acquit. Clearly God expects those who receive mercy to show mercy, especially toward those over whom one has authority or advantage. Grace is closely related to mercy, and the word for grace in the original biblical text gets translated into English in various ways, as mercy, lovingkindness, or goodness.

The specific meaning of grace as an attribute of God, however, is the willingness to bestow divine favor. Thus grace, like love, is a divine characteristic that always has an object or recipient. Grace also has a specific objective, which is redemption. Its purpose is to bestow upon the recipient the power to please God, most expressly in our manner of dealing with others. Grace is divinity endowing humanity with power to love. Human beings cannot directly emulate or reciprocate God's grace in this sense. Furthermore, it is impossible for us to assume a posture from which we can show favor to God. Rather, the human manifestation of grace is a quality of ease and elegance in doing what pleases God that signifies one's status as a recipient of divine favor. The signs of grace have little to do with sex, race, or economic status; instead, they indicate success in pleasing God.

To be holy is to be separate or set apart, and the very concept of holiness derives from the perception that there exists a divine reality that is "other" than everyone and everything that is. Worship is a reverent response to this sense of otherness. Holiness is God's premier attribute because of all the attributes discussed here holiness is the one most expressly characteristic of who God is. Each of these attributes reflects some aspect of God's holiness: creation is the institution and manifestation of God's holy order; love is God's holy will; God's holy word is truth; righteousness is God's holy way; mercy is God's holy compassion; and God's holy power is mediated by grace to accomplish God's purpose in the world. Applied to persons, the terms "holy" and "holiness" denote being set apart for God's service. God's people are holy because God is holy.

Unity and Holiness: Ethics for the People of God

Based upon our theological understanding of God's creativity, love, truth, righteousness, mercy, grace, and holiness, we can designate a corresponding ethics for the people of God that advocates unity and holiness. The fundamental conviction that directs this constructive process is the belief that to be ethical is to emulate a God who is creative, loving, truthful, righteous, merciful, gracious, and holy.

When God created humankind, God blessed them and spoke the very first commandment to "be fruitful and increase in number" (Gen. 1:28). Although the intent of this initial commandment is procreation, the continuing provision God makes for all dimensions of life, both physical and spiritual, issues not only in physical offspring but also spiritual fruit. Thus for the believer, the life of the spirit is a fruitful existence, where the inevitable by-product of the indwelling Holy Spirit is love, joy, peace, patience, kindness, goodness, faithfulness, gentleness, and self-control (Gal. 5:22-23). It is in this regard that we show our most intimate connection with the One who created us, that the divine creative process continues to replicate positive values and virtues in us. This spiritual fruit is holy because it comes from God, and it serves God's exclusive purposes in our lives and relationships. Yet there is another sense in which the commandment to be fruitful is fulfilled in the life of the believer. The church increases in number as fruitful Christians bear spiritual offspring, i.e., by evangelizing and discipling persons into fellowship with Jesus Christ. The realization that human beings were created by one Creator and blessed for fruitful partnership with one another leads to the conclusion that from the beginning holiness and unity are established as dominant objectives in God's plan for human existence.

While the fact of creation binds us all into one human family, it is love that identifies us as children of God. The covenant relationship God offers requires us to commit ourselves to active concern for others in response to how God has first loved us. All who enter into covenant on God's terms are bound to love one another, and to own each other as brother and sister. This notion of love has a quite different basis than the love we are obligated to show to neighbors and enemies without the expectation of return.

It is a familial bond with God as the one parent of a diverse array of siblings of all classes, colors, and cultures. Furthermore, it is a love that we ought to expect to be returned and shared and increased among all those who

identify themselves with the family of God. This covenant
that gives form and shape to the church is itself a commitment to holiness and unity; the sole measure of its validity
before God is our corporate and individual record of embrac-
ing as family those who share our commitment and reaching
out with concern for those who may not.

Love is the validation of our Christian identity, but truth
is what authorizes and authenticates it. Since God gave
existence to everyone and everything that is, God is the
source of all truth and the unity of all knowledge. Therefore
truth brings unity to the body of believers who are committed
to live in its light. Ethically speaking, we are challenged not
only to speak the truth, but also to employ the truth in
exposing the lies and deception that plague our existence in
the world.

Perhaps the most difficult aspect of truthfulness, the
reason why we often find silence or complicity more comfortable than truth-telling, is our fear of being subjected ourselves to moral scrutiny. In order to promote the truth, we
must simultaneously accept its full authority in every aspect
of our own lives. The light that was intended to dispel the
darkness should not be obscured by the moral laxity and
stubborn self-centeredness of unenlightened Christians.
Clearly, the prophetic dimension of the ministry to which we
are called is worthless and impotent in the absence of truth.
To advocate holiness and unity with integrity, we must
ourselves be united in holiness. We must understand that
holiness is the practical application of God's truth to our
daily living and that unity is the corporate spirit of the
children of light.

As an ethical principle, righteousness means conformity to
what is right. The root meaning of the word *righteous* is
"right way." For Christians, the right way is God's way, as
revealed in God's Word. Righteousness includes our attitudes, actions, and motives. In the individual righteousness
is virtue; in the society it is justice. Thus, individual unright-
eousness and social injustice both are manifestations of sin.
The manner in which justice is administered, particularly in

cases involving the poor and the disinherited, is a sure measure of the "rightness" of society's attitudes, actions, and motives. Individual righteousness is imputed by grace that we appropriate by faith; none can achieve righteousness apart from God. But social justice occurs not as an act of grace, but when righteous individuals work and advocate for it. One of the most costly moral errors made by Christians throughout human history is to divorce righteousness from justice, in assent to the idea that righteous individuals can tolerate and thrive in an unjust society with impunity, without addressing its evils or attempting in any way to change it. The interests of righteousness and justice are served when holy people unite to pursue God's way in the social order.

Mercy is the initiative taken to relieve suffering or forgive offenses with a primary concern for showing compassion. If justice is blind, mercy has eyes to see, ears to hear, and a heart to feel the pain of another. The imperative to show mercy is based on the fact that everyone benefits from the mercies of God. We must show mercy because we have received mercy. Mercy involves taking risks, such as the possibility that an offender will use acquittal as a springboard for further injustice, or that merciful acts will foster a debilitating pattern of dependency in those who otherwise might be moved to take responsibility for their own needs. Even greater risks may come into play, however, when we refuse to show mercy in the interest of protecting ourselves from danger or abuse, resulting in hardened hearts bereft of the capacity to care. In any case, justice must be balanced with mercy and compassion administered conscientiously in the fear of God. We must at all costs avoid the moral tragedy of using our zeal for righteousness as a justification for depriving others of needed help. The cause of unity and holiness is helped, and not hindered, by persons who are moved with conscientious compassion in their dealings with those who for whatever reason cannot help themselves.

Grace is a two-fold gift of God. By grace we receive salvation through the forgiveness of sin and sanctification as empowerment to serve. As beneficiaries of God's grace, the people of God are enabled to choose what is right in order to please God. Just as the graceful athlete or artist is one who effortlessly undertakes a difficult performance with ease and beauty, the effect of grace in the life of the believer is love, mercy, forgiveness, and every good work readily coming forth under the divine unction of the Spirit of God. The experience of salvation initiates and unites us into fellowship with all believers who have received God's saving grace. The experience of sanctification takes us beyond initiation to identity as children of God who graciously accept God's complete authority in our lives. Thus salvation and sanctification can be seen as personal experiences of grace that lead us to affirm holiness and unity as desirable attributes of our corporate life as members of God's church.

Just as holiness permeates and reflects all of the other attributes of God, it ought also to dominate the ethics and life-style of the people of God. In summary, the norms of holiness ethics as informed by our seven theological presuppositions concerning God are these: fruitfulness, in a manner consistent with God's original creative purpose for humankind; love, because God is love; truthfulness with integrity; righteousness with a godly zeal for justice; conscientious compassion, always bearing in mind the mercies God has extended to us; forgiveness, in humble acknowledgment that our salvation and sanctification are gifts of grace; and willingness to be especially set apart for service to God. In the Church of God tradition, the life-style concerns that follow from these norms include personal considerations such as abstinence from addictive substances such as alcohol, nicotine, and other harmful drugs; strict observance of the marriage covenant as the exclusive context for sexual activity; rejection of forms of entertainment that glorify lust and other ungodly passions; and modesty in dress. However, the biblical holiness tradition (which incidentally does not directly address drug use and some other life-style issues that are peculiar to our times) is centered upon ethical standards such as love, truth, justice, and mercy that illumine the "setting apart" of people for partnership with God and with each other in the work of reconciliation and redemption. In

141

this regard, holiness is more than personal piety or quiet asceticism; it is a bold and aggressive witness to the world, energized by a prophetic zeal for righteousness.

Sex, Race, and Sanctification

The privileged status of the white male in the Church of God is seriously called into question in view of the ethics of holiness and unity. If holiness is our method, and unity is our goal, then our ethical practices ought to be governed by the fruitfulness, love, truthfulness, righteousness, compassion, and forgiveness that set us apart as holy people of a holy God. A system that reserves the vast majority of pastoral and administrative leadership positions in the church for white men not only deviates from the principles of holiness and unity, but reveals a stubborn allegiance to sexism and racism. Such a system perpetuates itself by providing role models and support networks for white men who desire to serve, in effect excluding and discouraging those who are not white or male from aspiring to be trained and employed as leaders.

The sexist and racist practices within the Church of God are not only in evidence in the pulpits and agency offices, but in the local congregations as well. Most of our congregations are strictly segregated by race, and effectively proscribe the roles and influence of female members. To "reach our hands in fellowship to every bloodwashed one" is our song but not our practice, because we prefer to embrace those who are of our same race and class. While women may be gladly received into the fellowship, their ministries are often regarded as subordinate and auxiliary to the ministry of males.

Thankfully, some notable exceptions do exist to this pattern of racial segregation and sexist subordination within the leadership and fellowship of the Church of God, but they are too few. The practice of white male privilege not only contradicts our holiness and unity teaching, but reveals what many of our people really believe, namely, that people who are not white or males are inferior, and that it is appropriate to judge and discriminate among them on that basis. The extent to which Church of God people have assimilated the destructive racist and sexist ideas of the society is alarming, especially in view of the fact that we claim to serve a holy and just God. Instead of modeling for the world a community of faith whose witness is enriched and expanded by openness to all the people whom God has called and equipped for service, the Church of God mirrors the blasphemous duplicity of a society that proclaims that all are created equal, but excludes certain groups from access to justice and opportunity. This state of affairs is blasphemous insofar as it is grounded in the belief that God favors the white male, who alone bears God's image.

The Church of God reformation movement has not always embraced and practiced the racist and sexist biases of American culture. The nineteenth-century pioneers, zealous in their advocacy of holiness and unity, largely welcomed the full participation of women and blacks in the body of Christ during a time when racial and sexual discrimination was legally sanctioned and widely practiced in all sectors of the society. Their vision that the Spirit calls and equips the saints without respect to racial, sexual, or sectarian boundaries enabled them to reject both racial segregation and sexual subordination as inappropriate practices for God's church. With the rise of Jim Crow segregation in the South, however, and the demise of progressive evangelical feminism in other regions of the nation, Church of God leaders began to accommodate themselves to these shifting currents of social sentiment against blacks and women. This process of accommodation to the prevailing racist and sexist ethos of American society set the stage for two developments that have shaped the life of the Church of God in the twentieth century; the founding of the National Association of the Church of God, and the gradual retrenchment of women from the ranks of ordained ministry.

Blacks organized separate camp meetings and congregations because white racism essentially forced them out of fellowship with whites. The experience of women has been somewhat different, given the fact that they were excluded from leadership and not from fellowship. Instead of forming separate contexts for ministry and worship, women tended to accept subordinate status within the church, and women leaders largely have been relegated to roles as missionaries and teachers. Ironically, black women have been subjected to dual discrimination within the Church of God—as women, they have not had equal opportunity to assume leadership positions in black congregations or within the National Association; as blacks, they have been prejudged as unfit for fellowship and service in white congregations and agency offices. In ethical and historical perspective, then, the Church of God has retreated over time from a progressive vision of unity and equality in the body of Christ to a reactionary conformity to the discriminatory divisiveness of the society.

The hurts experienced by women and minorities who have been denied full partnership within the body of Christ will remain unhealed as long as the Church of God continues to accommodate itself to a sexist and racist society. The ignorant insensitivity of persons who have perpetuated exclusivity within the church in the interest of the preservation of privilege will continue to foster division and strife within the church if left unchecked. What is needed is a recall of the redeemed to examine the second blessing in light of the ethics of holiness and unity.

Sanctification is more than pious adherence to a select list of dos and don'ts—it is covenantal empowerment to serve God. The doctrine of sanctification proclaims that by the grace of God we can live free from sin. Our understanding of the sin from which we have been delivered, however, tends to be much too narrow, as measured by the degree of segregation and discrimination that exists within our congregations and national organizations. Since sin is manifested both in personal and social matters, so our sanctification from sin has both personal and social effects. To attend to personal concerns such as sexuality and dress without at the same time acknowledging our responsibility to overcome sin in the social order (e.g., racism, sexism, economic exploitation) is to assume the same dubious moral posture as the scribes and Pharisees whom Jesus rebuked, saying:

> You give to God one tenth even of the seasoning
> herbs, such as mint, dill, and cumin, but you neglect
> to obey the really important teachings of the Law,
> such as justice and mercy and honesty. These you
> should practice, without neglecting the others (Mt.
> 23:23, TEV).

When more individuals and congregations within the
Church of God begin to take seriously the relationship
between sanctification and social change, then the barriers
of sexual and racial division can be dismantled, the needed
healing and reconciliation can take place, and exciting new
applications of the ethics of holiness and unity to the divine
task of united ministry to a divided world can emerge.

We will conclude this chapter with a few suggestions
about how the ethical norms that reflect our commitment to
holiness and unity can redirect our responses to sexual and
racial diversity within the Church of God.

The fruitfulness to which we have been called by a creative
God begins with men and women coming together as faithful
partners and good stewards of God's creation. Our congregations will grow spiritually and numerically if we faithfully
model and promote the quality of partnership in ministry
and service that celebrates diversity in the pursuit of unity.

We are identified as Christians by our love. One way of
expressing our love as active concern is by evangelism that
openly encourages persons of both sexes and all races to
enter into covenant relationship as one family of one God.

Our witness to the world is authenticated by our commitment to truth. But, there can be little integrity in a church
that compromises God's truth by complicity with racial and
sexual discrimination. Since sin entered the world by the
denial of the truth, reconciliation can begin when we take
the bold step of speaking the truth in love.

The servants of a just and righteous God must be consistent in our own just action and righteous living. How we
apply justice in our organizational and institutional life is a

critical measure of our own righteousness. We must at least make every effort to be fair and impartial in our decisions, without being swayed by racial or sexual prejudices. We must always bear in mind that God judges individuals according to one standard of righteousness, and nations by the administration of justice to the poor and disinherited.

Ministries of mercy and compassion are greatly needed within the church, particularly ministries to be directed toward women and children who have been hurt by sexual discrimination and abuse. The task of ushering whites from racial insensitivity to acceptance requires a special quality of compassion, as does the complementary task of offering healing to those who have been the victims of racist acts and attitudes.

Closely related to the need for mercy is the need for means of offering and receiving forgiveness in the church. By our acceptance of God's grace we are saved and sanctified. However, the "saints" must be reminded from time to time that the church is a forgiving community, and that we must allow grace to bring forth the spiritual fruit in our lives that will bless others in turn. Genuine unity among persons of different sexes, classes, and cultures is only made possible by grace.

Our testimony of holiness can be totally invalidated by the practice of prejudice. Being set apart for God's exclusive use means that we resist conformity to worldly standards that devalue others on the basis of race and sex, and we reject all forms of discrimination and oppression. Thus, personal transformation that we experience as sanctification also fits us for engagement in social change.

Juanita Evans Leonard

Juanita Leonard is an ordained minister of the Church of God. She is Associate Professor of Church and Society in the School of Theology at Anderson University. She is also Associate Secretary with Women of the Church of God for Cross Cultural Issues.

Leonard served as Pastor of Family Life Ministries as a staff member at the Church of the Crossing, Indianapolis, Indiana. She has a Masters degree in Social Service from Indiana University and a Post Graduate Certificate in Marriage and Family counseling from the University of Minnesota. In 1986, she received the Distinguished Service Award from the American Association of Marriage and Family Therapists.

She has a Masters degree in Missiology from Fuller Theological Seminary, Pasadena, California. She served in Cross Cultural Missions with the Mennonite Central Committee in Kenya, East Africa. This ministry involved Family Life Education Programming.

Her writings have appeared in Vital Christianity, Christian Leadership, *and pamphlets for the Evangel Publishing Company, Kenya, East Africa.*

Chapter 9:

Women, Change, and the Church

Juanita Evans Leonard

I n earlier chapters specific biblical, theological, and historical data regarding the empowerment and leadership of women in the Church of God have been given. These life stories and ethical concerns of ministry have been lifted up to point the way for further discussion and exploration.

Leadership issues facing the church as she moves into the twenty-first century will be discussed in this chapter. The role of women in this broader concern will be explored with suggested strategies for intentional change of the status quo. The diagnoses and strategies for change are offered as ideas for prayer, discussion, and action on the part of women and men who are called to "Go into all the world preaching, teaching. . . ."

Relationships

The closing lines of the familiar marriage service end with the words "to preserve an inviolable fidelity, and to see to it, that what God has joined thus together, man never puts asunder" (Hiscox 1878, 215).

Paul writing to the Christians in Rome said:

> "With eyes wide open to the mercies of God, I beg you, my brothers, as an act of intelligent worship, to give him your bodies, as a living sacrifice, consecrated to him and acceptable by him. Don't let the world around you squeeze you into its own mold, but let God remold your minds from within so that the plan of God for you is good, meets all his demands and moves toward the goal of true maturity" (Phillips 1958, 341).

The lesson in both of these admonitions speak of that which could cause either a man or woman not to fulfill the purpose of God in his/her life. The first speaks of a human relationship, a social institution central to the human family. The second, a spiritual reality, which permeates believers' realities of life in the world. It would appear that the claim of God on our life and our commitment to the call of God must be diligently and persistently obeyed or the potential of a "mess of pottage" will result. The Church as a social institution stands in grave danger should it persist in disallowing either consciously or unconsciously the giftedness of women in the total life of the Church. The structure of the Church as well as every pastoral responsibility must include women's giftedness. The lack of women's full presence in all dimensions of the Church's life has been manifested over and over in the history of faith communities who were in their beginning open to women exercising all the spiritual gifts—apostles, teachers, administrators, helps, mercy. As the group became organized, the structures began to look like the social institutions in the culture. The Church adopted society's structural norms. "Our recorded heritage reveals that there have always been women preachers in the Church of God. They are accepted without debate. We have had decades when our culture influenced our Movement to discourage women in pastoral ministry" (McCutcheon 1980, 5).

Women and men who are convinced of the message of Holiness in Acts 1 and 2 would be in agreement with Kari

Torgensen Malcolm writing about the mid-nineteenth century holiness revivals.

> Because of the emphasis on declaring what God has done, silence became almost a sin, as Phoebe Upham suggests: "To impart what one receives from God is the outgoing life of the new Christ nature. . . . How opposed then to the new Christ nature, and to God's word, is the sealing of woman's lips in the public exercises of the Church" (Malcolm 1982, 127).

D.S. Warner, like John Wesley, Charles G. Finney, and Phoebe Palmer, emphasized the sanctification of the Holy Spirit on the believer's life. Pentecost was central to the experience of holiness. Believers expected to be empowered with gifts to witness with "holy boldness" to the end that the good news would convince men and women of sin and the reconciliation of brokenness would be experienced.

Church historian John W.V. Smith wrote:

> There was never a time in the history of the movement in fact, when women were not considered an essential part of the leadership. It was a striking aspect of the early days to see women functioning on the same level as men. Forty years before the time of woman's suffrage on a national level a great company of women were preaching, singing, writing and helping to determine the policies in this religious reform movement (Smith 1955, 125).

In 1902, *Familiar Names and Faces* was published. A list of fifty women appeared of the two hundred leaders in the first generation of the history of the Church of God Reformation Movement. By the time the suffrage movement had gained momentum the numbers of women acknowledged as pastoral leaders was 32 percent. In the first two decades of the twentieth century, however, the charismatic (dynamic) nature of leadership changed. Agency structures emerged and the professionalization process of clergy set in. The advance made by women was being lost. Statistics reported

151

by Sharon Sawyer's research gives some indication of the process (Sawyer 1976, 2).

Year	Number of congregations	Number of Women Pastors	Percentage of congregations with women pastors
1905	353	50	14%
1925	685	220	32%
1945	1572	112	7%
1965	2276	100	4%
1975	2905	100	3%

The next fifty years of the Church were indeed bleak for women. As the institutional structures of the reform movement developed, the doors once open to women became only cracks. The dominant cultural forms persisted and were exacerbated following World War II. Women had managed the places men had filled during this war as had been done during World War I. At the war's end women were obliged to go back into what some have called "the feminine mystique." Malcolm suggests it was a "longing of society to go back to the 'good ole days'" (Malcolm 1982, 137).

Diagnosis: From Pain to Problems to Change

Questions must be asked about the years 1925 to 1975. The press of the world's mold was overtaking the movement. It is not possible to speak of women's leadership in the church during this part of its history without talking about racism. Black men and women as well as white women were marginalized in the larger society and in the church. Writing about the sociological development of the Church of God in *Where the Saints Have Trod,* Clear has said:

> In its early years the sect often grows phenomenally, because it offers dramatic answers to questions which deeply bother potential adherents. But in the process of answering the questions it tends to produce conditions which diminish its sectarian form. Created to fill a pressing need, the sect meets the need success-

152

fully, and in doing so it makes itself obsolete. In most cases, of course, the negativistic sect-form gives way to accommodation patterns, so that the organization continues to serve the same group of people, developing new institutional forms as the needs of the people change. Starting as a conflict group, it ultimately becomes an accommodating group (Clear 1977, 3).

Anthropologist/Missiologist Paul Hiebert writes, "Institutions, like people, go through cycles of growth, maturation, and 'hardening of the categories.' The result often is a loss of vitality and life they once had" (Hiebert 1986, 112).

Women had received the franchise to vote in 1920 and there was every hope that participation in the political arena also meant that society was ready for women in all spheres of activity. History records that changes did not come so quickly and the church reflected the society. The *Gospel Trumpet,* a Church of God periodical, recorded activities of women on the overseas mission field, but there were few references to activities of women in the United States. Women evangelists were becoming few in number. There were the exceptions like Mother Emma Meyer (1894-1920) of Louisville, Kentucky, Birdie Smith (1932-1946) of Akron, Ohio, Minna Jarrett (1937-1957) of Vancouver, Washington, and Lillie McCutcheon (1947-1989) Newton Falls, Ohio, who were pastors of established congregations. Hiebert describes the process of institutionalization:

> First, the founding parents of an institution often pay a high price to join it, and take personal risk. They join together in a bond or fellowship of high intensity, and tremendous purpose and fellowship. The second generation is raised inside the organization and this makes them radically different. To stay in is the easiest course with little sacrifice. Nevertheless they experience vicariously the commitment and vision of their parents and often have a high commitment to the institution. The third generation is more

removed from the founders and has less of their vision. Nominalism enters, and many stay in because it is the course of least resistance. The result is a growing loss of interest, a shift in goals and institutionalization. The fourth generation and on are well entrenched and the institution for them is a way of life. They have much invested in it in terms of their own identity and want to maintain it not for what it does in ministry for the world, but what it does for them as persons (Hiebert 1986, 113).

The next forty years saw the third and fourth generations of leaders emerge. Early in the sixties, "the feminine mystique" was being recognized by some women. The Civil Rights movement was in full swing and the nation was embroiled in a turbulent war in Southeast Asia. There was ferment in the land and women reared in the Church of God, who had heard the call of God on their lives, found the church unresponsive to their gifts. Women took the work of love and reconciliation of Jesus into other settings. The union halls, social work agencies, hospitals, and educational institutions both at home and overseas were their pulpits and places of service. While the cities of the United States burned, women began to ask difficult questions of the church. Because lay women and those few ordained (by the institutional church) knew that their "service" had been rooted in the "hearing of the word," from the pulpits of the very church that now had no place for them, began to once more "cry out" as Nora Hunter did in an earlier generation.

The routinization of the Church of God, the social milieu of the day, and the empowerment by the Holy Spirit helped to create a renewed vision of the place of women in the leadership of the church. What had transpired in the Church of God had been documented in the life of other communions of faith within the Holiness traditions. Nancy Hardesty writes: "Holiness and Pentecostal groups, however, became preoccupied with institution building—churches, denominational structures, publishing houses, colleges, even seminaries. In the beginning they despised seminary-educated ministries;

now they coveted one for their own congregation. Begun often as churches of the urban poor, they [women] were again squeezed out of leadership by the values of the dominant culture. They were evangelists and missionaries, home and foreign, but they were not pastors of larger churches, denominational executives, or seminary professors" (Hardesty 1984, 159).

Vision had given way to routine. This was particularly true of the grass roots of the organization. Self-maintenance was substituted for evangelization and the healing of the ills of people and society. Vested interest in maintaining the institution emerged with identities and rewards tied up in the process along with these roles and statuses within it. More effort was spent on maintaining the organization and less on ministry to the world. Flexibility had given way to inflexibility. The ray of hope for women throughout the forty year period, 1920 to 1960, was the emergence of the lay Womens Missionary Society.

A change of name for the Womens Missionary Society came in 1974. The Women of the Church of God were a vast untapped leadership potential for the *life* of the church. Some of its strength lay in the fact that it was outside of the hierarchical "family of agencies." Led during the late sixties and seventies by an ordained minister, Nellie J. Snowden and the staff working with her (Marie Meyer, Joyce Nisely, Johanna Bridges, Nell McManus, and Kay Shively) this grass roots network of women helped shape questions about women. What were women doing with God's call on their lives? Why were women not part of the decision-making bodies of the Church? Why were women not being invited by congregations to be pastors? The questioners also wanted to know if women were entering the church colleges and seminary in preparation for the ministry. In 1971, Barry Callen, faculty member of Bible and Religion Department of Anderson University, questioned the absence of women in the School of Theology. (See appendices.)

The categories of the organization had been hardened! The focus on people had given way to focus on programs.

Success was measured in programs and buildings. As the institutional machinery grew, white women and ethnic minorities were increasingly detached and alienated from the Church. The core composition of the "Flying Ministries" was gone. Impersonalization was rampant and the majority clergy controlled the institution. When the daring women in ministry began to raise the penetrating questions, people had become more interested in what they could get out of the institution rather than what they could contribute to it. The church was no longer sensitive to women's needs and goals in service. The egalitarian informality of the beginnings had given way to the growing hierarchy. The sense of camaraderie as "the whole people of God" had died and power controlled the institution. The intellectual assent to women in ministry was present but the realized vision once more had to be "fanned into flame" by the Holy Spirit's power and those empowered by the Word.

The women and men who were advocates for women in leadership had challenged a small minority of women within the church. Women of the Movement slowly, haltingly at times, began to name the questions more boldly. Many did not wish to admit the controlling nature of the institution and the closed doors to women in ministry. By the Spirit's power over and over again, the renewal process of the church began and women started finding their voice.

In 1973, Women of the Church of God conducted a conference in cooperation with the Division of Church Service during the International Convention. Statistics given about the role of women within the various structures of the Church were given. They called the church to accountability. The General Assembly passed a resolution in 1974 urging that more women be given consideration for positions of leadership in the total program of the Church of God. Although the resolution was weak, it did add to the renewed hope for women in ministry.

The Commission on Social Concerns was directed to monitor the process under the guidance of Edward Foggs, Associate Executive Secretary of the Executive Council.

During the Commission meeting of 1976 a motion was introduced that a survey be developed that would profile what the congregations were doing in social concerns.

The questionnaire was developed and facilitated by the Commission on Social Concerns, Women of the Church of God, and the Division of Church Service. It was then sent to each church in the yearbook of the Church of God. Table 2 provides some clarification of the roles women were assuming during the mid-seventies.

Role of Women within Church of God Structures, 1973

	Number of Women	Number of Men
Pastoring	71	505
Leading Worship	666	998
Board of Trustees	580	1094
Church Council	1417	1538
Board of Deacons	135	282
Pastors Advisory Committees	342	207
Other Major Committees	1418	952
Membership on State Committees	277	322

The Division of Church Service reported in the *1976 Yearbook of American and Canadian Churches* 276 women as being ordained. Women were being resourced on local levels. But the statistics pointed to a glaring gap when considering the number of women in pastoral leadership and those serving on major boards, agencies, and institutions of higher education.

Two hundred eleven women were ordained into ministry from 1967 to 1987. Comparing this number with other communions of faith who also ordain women, the Church of God moved from tenth to fourteenth in number of women clergy out of twenty-one denominations reporting from 1976 to 1986. The Table below prompted several questions.

Women Clergy in 21 U.S. Denominations, 1977-1986

Denomination	No. 1977	1977 Rank	No. 1986	1986 Rank	Gain/ Loss	% of Inc./ Dec.
American Baptist Churches	157	(11)	429	(10)	+272	173
American Lutheran Churches*	18	(16)	306	(12)	+288	1,600
Assemblies of God	1,572	(2)	3,718	(1)	+2,146	136
Christian Church (Disciples of Christ)	388	(6)	743	(7)	+355	91
Christian Congregation	125	(12)	290	(13)	+165	132
Church of God (Anderson, Ind.)	272	(10)	275	(14)	+3	1
Church of the Brethren	27	(15)	120	(16)	+93	344
Church of the Nazarene	426	(4)	355	(11)	-71	-17
Episcopal Church	94	(13)	796	(6)	+702	747
Free Methodist Church	11	(17)	69	(17)	+58	527
International Church of the Foursquare Gospel	804	(3)	666	(8)	-138	-17
Lutheran Church in America*	55	(14)	484	(9)	+429	780
Mennonite Church	4	(18)	48	(18)	+44	1,100
Mennonite Church, The General Conference	4	(18)	33	(20)	+29	725
Moravian Church (Unitas Fratrum)	3	(20)	16	(21)	+13	433
Presbyterian Church (U.S.A.)**	(370)	(8)	1,519	(4)	+1,149	310
Reformed Church in America	1	(21)	42	(19)	+41	+4100
Salvation Army	3,037	(1)	3,220	(2)	+183	6
United Church of Christ	400	(5)	1,460	(5)	+1,060	265
United Methodist Church	319	(9)	1,891	(3)	+1,572	+493
Wesleyan Church	384	(7)	255	(15)	-129	-33
	8,471		16,735		+8,264	+98

*These bodies and the Association of Evangelical Lutheran Churches merged to form The Evangelical Lutheran Church in America which began operations on January 1, 1988.

**Data for 1977 are for The United Presbyterian Church in the U.S.A. and the Presbyterian Church in the U.S. that merged in 1983.

(*Eculink* No. 20, September 1988)

Gilbert Stafford of the Anderson School of Theology asked, "What is influencing the faith communities on the issue of women in ministry?" If the truth in scripture were being implemented by the institutional church when it speaks of women and men being gifted for ministry in equipping the church for service, then the question had to be raised— what is blocking the dynamism revealed through scripture?

Stafford also observed, "The Assemblies [of God], which is still very much in touch with its pentecostal hermeneutic, shows a significant increase whereas the Wesleyan Church and the Church of the Nazarene, which are now being greatly influenced by a legalistic interpretation of Paul, show a significant decline" (Stafford, unpublished memo to faculty of School of Theology, 1988).

Perhaps the Church of God has drifted away from her hermeneutic of scripture. Callen's words of 1971 echoed in the ears of many, "Men normally change direction only when adequate force is applied to compel the change. Institutions are usually static and men are usually stubborn." Closing his remarks Callen added, "Why are not more women now entering the Church of God ministry, the School of Theology? Is it as Constance Parvey suggests, because of (a) the subtle attitudinal opposition of men and (b) female perception that, more than other socially oriented professions which they are going into, the Christian ministry is characterized by a social conservatism bordering on professional irrelevance: Do we need new programs and new image in order to attract the "fair" sex into Christian Ministry?" (1971, unpublished paper).

Women responded then and do today to the question of programs by saying no! New programs are not the basic need. Women simply want the organizational church to act upon the revealed scripture as the way the church throughout its structures should function. *Obey* what the Spirit has revealed and given. Use all the gifts that women have for the work of the Kingdom. Women have wanted nothing more than to be taken seriously. They want the relevance of the Word to be actualized in the hearts and minds and ministries of the church so that a divided world would know that Jesus Christ is Lord! The egalitarian words and ministry of Jesus is the foundation. It is not a passive spiritual notion. It is a living reality that is countercultural to the institutional nature of hierarchical structures. The "word" lived out would mean that the home and family and the life of the Church would know a reality like that in Jesus' day. The time is now; the issue is urgent.

159

The Executive Council in 1984 called a Consultation on Ministry and Mission toward the year 2000. This consultation brought together 150 men and women representing the major cultural groups served by the Church. *Direction Toward the Year 2000* stated: Women are being called trained, ordained for ministry but few are called to local pastorates. Goal number 12.3 of the report says that one of the steps that needs to be taken by the Church is "to enable the Church of God to accept the ministry of women in pastoral and other leadership roles." The report continues to call for the development of a process for involving state, provincial, and area assemblies in promoting models of servant leadership after those of Christ.

The focus of the 1984 Consultation concerning women in ministry gave direction to the School of Theology to develop a consultation of and for women clergy. The consultation planned by women was to help implement what women had long been saying. It has taken five years to bring this directive to fruition. A grant from the Women of the Church of God enabled the School of Theology to convene a two-day working group of eleven theologians, pastors, educators, and missionaries. These women prayed about and talked about the role of women in ministry for the last decade of the twentieth century and beyond. They discussed the question of what could be done to change the course of Church of God history regarding the dearth of women in leadership positions. The results of the February 1988, St. Louis, Missouri, gathering was the planning of the first Consultation on Women in Ministry and Mission in the 110 year history of the Church. The idea and outline for this volume was birthed by this group of women. The vision of what could be is being blessed by the Spirit.

Late in 1988 a fifteen-year study on the trends of ministerial leadership was published. This study by Jerry Grubbs, past Dean of the School of Theology, states that 3,300 ordained clergy are registered in the *1988 Yearbook of the Church of God.*

Ordained Pastors	1,553	(47%)
Ordained Retired	668	(20%)
Ordained Ministers	339	(10%)
Ordained Associates	263	(8%)
Ordained (Various)	477	(15%)

The statistics did not show the need and demand for specialized ministries such as chaplains, missionaries, counselors, teachers, and others (Grubbs 1988, 3). There are no statistics available indicating the death of clergy or loss from ministry of those who are burned out or leave for moral reasons. Grubbs calls the church to consider the commitment of starting 770 new churches in the last 12 years of the century. Where will the leadership come from? This is his summation of need:

1. Present congregations not served by a pastor   632
2. Persons reaching retirement by year 2000   630
3. New church planters needed to reach goal   770
4. Growth in need for associate pastors   240
5. Need for specialized dropouts   120
6. Replacement for dropouts   60
7. Death of pastors   60
Potential need toward year 2000   2,512
(Table 3, (Grubbs 1988, 4)

Is now the time for the use of women's gifts on a major scale? It is obvious that Grubbs' findings would indicate that not only is our hermeneutic in question but the leadership crisis is not understood by the majority of the church. The lack of qualified leadership is staggering. There is a felt need on the part of some leadership. Is this lack of leadership and the decline in the majority culture churches any indication to the church that now is the time for implementing change and noting the gifts of women? Is the inclusion of women on the agenda at all levels of the institution?

The following table indicates some of the positions to which women could be called to use their gifts.

The following statistical information is given for the number of women in agency positions with titles of executive secretary, associate secretary, president, vice president, executive director, director, and board member. The statistics were taken from the 1980, 1983, 1986, 1988, and 1989 yearbooks.

AGENCY	YEAR	POSITION		BOARD	
		#	Women	#	Women
Executive Council	1980	3	0	25	5
	1983	2	0	25	6
	1986	2	0	25	7
	1988	2	0	25	6
	1989	2	0	25	6
Church Service	1980	1	0	9	1
	1983	1	0	9	1
	1986	1	0	9	1
	1988	1	0	9	0
	1989	1	0	9	0
World Service	1980	5	0	18	1
	1983	5	0	19	2
	1986	5	0	19	2
	1988	6	0	19	3
	1989	5	0	19	2
Board of Christian Education	1980	6	1	15	4
	1983	6	1	15	5
	1986	6	1	15	5
	1988	5	1	15	6
	1989	6	1	15	7
Board of Church Extension and Home Mission	1980	14	1	21	3
	1983	13	1	21	3
	1986	16	1	21	4
	1988	15	1	21	5
	1989	5	0	21	5

Mass Communications	1980	1	0	11	1
	1983	2	0	11	2
	1986	1	0	11	2
	1988	2	0	11	2
	1989	1	0	11	2
Missionary Board	1980	5	0	15	4
	1983	6	2	20	5
	1986	7	2	20	4
	1988	5	2	20	5
	1989	2	0	20	5
Board of Pensions	1980	1	0	10	1
	1983	1	0	10	1
	1986	1	0	10	1
	1988	2	0	10	1
	1989	2	0	10	1
Warner Press	1980	5	0	25	5
	1983	5	0	25	4
	1986	6	0	25	4
	1988	5	0	25	4
	1989	3	0	25	4

SCHOOLS

Anderson University	1980	4	0	30	3
	1983	4	0	30	3
	1986	6	1	30	3
	1988	6	1	30	4
	1989	7	1	30	4
Warner Pacific	1980	4	0	26	4
	1983	6	0	27	4
	1986	5	1	25	4
	1988	6	0	25	4
	1989	6	0	25	3

Gulf Coast/					
Mid-America	1980	3	0	29	3
	1983	4	0	25	3
	1986	3	0	25	3
	1988	2	1	25	2
	1989	2	1	25	2
Bay Ridge	1980	3	0	26	4
	1983	3	1	26	4
	1986	2	0	24	3
	1988	2	0	24	2
	1989	2	0	24	2
Warner Southern	1980	7	0	25	0
	1983	6	0	25	0
	1986	6	0	25	0
	1988	3	0	25	0
	1989	3	0	26	1

(2/08/89—J.E. Leonard)

Is this the foregoing force that Callen wrote about in 1971? Lewin's force field research would indicate this to be true (see Schallers' *The Change Agents*). Is there still hope? Can the first decade of the second century of the Church of God provide a vision for the new century? Is it now possible to act intentionally upon the revealed truth found in the Book of Acts? The answer is a resounding yes! But to be not only *hearers* of the word but *doers* of the word is urgent. What is being called for is a reformation. Christ has broken down the walls of partition. Kenneth LaTourette, Mission Historian, wrote, "The Church's task is not to save itself; Christ has already done that. It is rather to give itself in love and service—in fact to die for the world" (LaTourette 1943). Women simply are calling the church to join them in this task.

What must be the response of the total church if we are to meet the challenge set before us not to simply maintain the institutional church and the dearth of leadership that is upon us, but to go beyond anything we could ever hope or dream?

Planned Change Culb- radical chg

The purpose of planned change in this chapter is the renewing of our minds with respect to the gifts of women called of God for pastoral leadership. In order to see this vision through to completion, it will take a radical countercultural decision to act upon the biblical imperatives.

When the structures of the institution fall—the walls of partition that block the creative use of women's spiritual gifts—it will be because the majority who influence the church have abandoned "ideas which are in accord with their interest, needs, or existing attitudes. . . . Consciously, or unconsciously, people avoid messages that are in conflict with our predispositions" (Rogers 1971, 105). This tendency has been called *selective exposure.* "People will seldom expose themselves to messages about innovation and change unless they first feel a need for the change. Even if persons are exposed to the innovative messages, Hassinger has argued, there will be little effect of such exposure unless the individual perceives the innovation relevant to his/her needs and as consistent with his/her existing attitudes or beliefs" (Rogers 1972, 105).

There is a need, a state of dissatisfaction or frustration, seen and felt on the part of women called to minister and men who are advocates for the use of women's gifts. The desire to serve outweighs the actualities of being free to serve as pastors, evangelists, decision makers on boards, agencies, and as staff of these groups.

To be a change agent for the leadership of women the following must be put into action:

> Identify the kinds of barriers that are most important to blocking women in ministry and the kind of filters that are used to maintain the system in the congregation, state assembly, or in the national agencies and offices;

> select and engage in dialogue with key members of your community (network) about the giftedness of women in the pastoral leadership of the church;

discuss the issues of women in leadership with those in your immediate network of friends; consider the need for pastoral leadership in the Church of God; discuss the biblical and historical foundation for the role of women in leadership;

call together the women and men within your church, state or region who are working with these concerns, and note the issues and the opportunities.

As the number of persons who are involved increases, the acceptance of leadership of women will begin to be actualized. The critical mass of key individuals will be taken seriously.

As change agents, it is important to remember the three types of people who will help you in getting the status quo to adopt the idea of women in ministry. They have been defined by various writers, such as Rogers, Havelock, Schaller, Smith, and Flikkema. For our purpose Havelock's work is most useful.

The *Innovators* are risk takers. They tend to be intelligent, are travelers, read a lot, use outside sources of information, and often are receptive to the influence of outside change agents.

The *Resisters* in most social systems (which includes the Church) have some members who take the active role as critics of innovation and/or change. Most often these persons are defenders of the system the way it is. Usually they are self-appointed guardians of the moral, ethical and legal standards. Although these people are "conservative" in a strictly logical sense, they may wear all kinds of labels from "radical" and "liberal" to "reactionary" (Havelock 1973, 120). Innovations such as integration, urban renewal, and floridation of community water supplies have been slowed down by resisters. Preservers of the social order, the resisters play a useful part. They resist alien influences in our society. The analogy of anti-bodies in the blood stream comes to mind when speaking of resisters. (73:120)

The *Leaders*—the opinion leaders play a significant role. These people are key to the use of women's leadership gifts. The opinion leaders are held in high esteem within the church nationally, regionally, and locally. They will have control of the power and money of the church. Most often these people are not the ones to try out the innovation because they need to stay in good standing with the majority. Opinion leaders are listeners to the innovators and resisters. They attempt to get a balanced understanding of the issue. It is certain that the opinion leaders are eager to observe the development of the issue because their ability to remain in *power* depends on the ability to judge innovations. These leaders wish to be champions of the innovations whose time has come.

The leadership of these opinion leaders may be formal, informal, administrative, or elective. Who are these leaders? They are the pastors, state and local presidents of the Women of the Church of God organizations, chairpersons of committees within the church, state, regional, and national church. State coordinators and executives of national agencies are central to leadership decisions. All the persons in the networks of relationships must be considered. The various opinion leaders act as legitimators, helping people feel good about the active role of women in ministry. There will be others who serve as facilitators or encouragers of the idea. The gatekeepers will be those who open up doors once closed to women.

Women, change, and the church are not static. The Spirit is guiding the vision of Christ for women to preach and teach. God's people can no longer disobey the revealed word by operating in the church with the world's values and restrictions of over half the church's adherents because of gender, race, economic status, physical handicap, or age.

Where the Spirit of the Lord is, there is peace, power, perseverance, and praise. God is raising up a "great company" of women in this generation, to take the message of holiness, unity, and love into all the world.

Appendix A

Women in the Ministry

by Barry L. Callen

To begin our discussion . . .

Getting Ourselves Together

Men normally change direction only when adequate force is applied to compel the change. Institutions are usually static and men are usually stubborn.

The hope is that these pessimistic (if not profound) pronouncements do not dominate the rationale behind or the possible fruits of the present discussion. The church is facing a crisis in the available quantity of trained leadership—which means that the pressure is building for change—change regarding any artificial limitations presently restricting new sources of leadership. Is this why we gather here today, to discuss reverting to women as one possible means of dissolving our dilemma? One hopes that it is more than that. Be it some modern movement for women's liberation or some ancient movement (like the Christian faith) that called for the most profound liberation of all "men," there is agreement that we shall disagree with St. Chrysostom's judgment that woman is merely "a necessary evil, a natural temptation, a domestic peril."

Why Are We Here?

1. To Look at the Situation

To confront the criticism that "Both Judaism and Christianity have incorporated the dominant patriarchal attitude of the culture of their origins, and tended to maintain the culture's superstitious attitude toward feminine 'uncleanness' and 'wickedness.' " —Douglas

Is it characteristic of our ecclesiastical thinking (Church of God) that "woman as wife and mother deserves respect and protection, but woman as leader, authority, and spokesman defies both Nature and Scripture?" What about our supreme allegiance to the authority of the Bible wherein one hears the "inspired" Apostle Paul insisting upon the auxiliary and subordinate function for women in the Church? St. Paul aside (or more adequately interpreted), should we in the church strive to encourage women to be "just the same as men"? What is the situation biblically and historically? What is the stake anyway? Where on the scale do we fall when the discussion turns to the psychological, biological, and theological reasons why women should or should not be limited in their level and type of ecclesiastical involvement?

2. To Plan a Strategy for the Future

We would likely all agree with Ann Mow that "the question is really not women with men in the ministry, or men only in the ministry; the question is, 'Is the message from the Lord?' and 'Is the Lord represented?' " Or, again, who would oppose James Pike's conclusion that "what is at stake is not just greater fulfillment in the lives of some women church members here and there. What is at stake is the sincerity of the church's profession that persons are to be treated as persons, not as anonymous components of a generic category, that is, as things." But just what will we do in the future based on these placid abstractions? What is the shape and scope of the leadership vacuum presently in the Church of God; what mindset seems to prevail regarding increased female participation in filling this vacuum; what responsibility has Anderson [University] and the School of Theology in speaking courageously and creatively to the vacuum and to the mind-set; what specifically can and should be done on this campus to set in motion the needed innovations?

Why are not more women now entering the Church of God ministry—the School of Theology? Is it, as Constance Parvey suggests, because of (a) the "subtle attitudinal opposition of men" and (b) female perception that, more than other socially oriented professions—which they are going into, the Christian ministry is characterized by a social conservatism bordering on professional irrelevance? Do we need new programs and new images in order to attract [women] into the Christian ministry?

Prepared by:

Barry L. Callen
February 10, 1971

Appendix B

Statistics of 1976 Survey by Executive Council of General Assembly of the Church of God

1. The total of congregations in the U.S. and Canada is 2300; total membership in these churches is approximately 250,000. Women make up about 55 percent of the membership.

2. Currently, the Yearbook lists 76 women as pastors and 29 women serving as Associate Ministers.

3. Women pastors are found working with the smaller churches, most with fewer than fifty members. Only one woman is pastor of a church with a membership of over 200.

4. Although our black membership is less than 12 percent of the total church, more black women serve as pastors than white.

5. 883 women in 921 churches serve on the Board of Trustees—fewer than one per church.

6. 2,995 women in 921 churches serve on the Church Council, slightly more than three per church.

7. 219 women are involved on state church board or organizations, approximately one woman to every four churches.

8. The smaller the church the more women are involved on decision-making bodies; the larger the church the fewer women involved. Rather, they are found in programming bodies, such as the Church Council.

9. The number of women on national boards and agencies (excluding the W.C.G. and the Men's fellowship) are 24. For men the number is 217.

This survey was done with a questionnaire sent to all pastors of the Church of God congregations. This information was furnished through the help and courtesy of the Church Service office. 921 churches responded to the questionnaire. These churches appear to fall into generally the same percentages concerning size and makeup as do the total of Church of God congregations.

Appendix C

Church of God Women Pastors:
A Look at the Statistics

by Susie Stanley

December 1988

Year	Congregations	Women Pastors	% Congregations Women Pastors
1895	353	50	14%
1915	487	85	17%
1920	464	92	19%
1925	685	220	32%
1930*	601	123	20%
1935	1326	121	9%
1940	1270	136	11%
1945	1572	112	7%
1950	1893	117	6%
1955	2095	133	6%
1960	2244	109	5%
1965	2276	100	4%
1970	2267	78	3%
1975	2905	100	3%
1980*	2259	78	3%
1985*	2271	59	2%

Discussions of women in ministry in the Church of God generally include comments on the dramatic decline of women pastors over the years. To my knowledge, no one has done a thorough analysis of ministerial statistics to document precisely the extent of the decline. In a 1976 article Sharon Sawyer presented partial data, which is reproduced above along with additional information as indicated (Sawyer 1976). The following are tentative observations based on these statistics.

Before focusing on the decline in women pastors, we should take note of the tremendous increase that occurred between 1920 and 1925 when the number of women pastoring more than doubled during this period of time. What accounts for this dramatic gain? Were women especially encouraged to consider pastoral ministry during this time? Were women transferring from evangelistic work to the pastorate? This was the case for Nora Siens Hunter. (See page 51 of this volume for a brief summary of Hunter's ministry.) If Hunter's experience is representative, the increase can be attributed partially to the transition from an emphasis on evangelistic work to the settled pastorate.

The largest decrease in the number of women pastors took place between 1925 and 1930 when the number dropped from 220 to 123, a loss of 97 women pastors. Again, this raises several questions. Were women discouraged from serving as pastors? Or was age a factor? Were the ranks of women pastors depleted due to deaths or retirement, or did women leave the pastorate to go into other areas of work? These questions cannot be answered definitively until the lives of individual women pastors are explored in more detail.

Joseph Allison attributes the decline in women pastors to the shift from the traveling evangelistic ministry to the focus on local congregations. This move affected women in at least two ways. First, as congregations began hiring pastors, "women found fewer openings for their evangelistic and church-planting gifts" (Allison, 1988, 9). Second, "The new situation cut off most opportunities for women to apprentice themselves to experienced ministers who were traveling and preaching" (Allison, 1978, 27). According to Allison, the decline in women pastors occurred when the women evangelists turned pastors died out and "there was no new generation of women evangelists to take their place" (Allison).

Others blame the decline in women pastors on the influence of cultural attitudes toward women. Rev. Lillie McCutcheon observed that while there have always been women preachers in the Church of God, "We have had decades when our culture influenced our movement to discourage women in pastoral ministry. . . . It is disappointing that the church continues to remain with male domination when it should have pioneered the equal status for women" (McCutcheon 1980, 5-6). Likewise, Harold Phillips points to the acceptance of women in the early years of the movement. He contrasts this with the situation in the 1970s when the Episcopal Church faced controversy over the ordination of women. However, he cautions, "But before we gather Pharisaic robes about ourselves, perhaps we need to look candidly at the way in which we, too, succumbed to some of the cultural and prejudicial patterns of later decades!" (Phillips 1978, 14). Allison pinpoints specific "watersheds" in his analysis of women ministers. He contends that World War I "brought more freedom and greater responsibility for women, while the second war period did just the opposite" (Allison, 1978, 27). The church capitulated to society's understanding of the role of women and began to conform to cultural stereotypes of "woman's place."

Allison writes: "From 1916 to 1940 women made notable advances in the Church of God because of the movement's basic openness to women leaders. It is only at the end of the period, during World War II, that we see women losing their grip upon the ministerial office" (Allison 1978, 28). I agree with Allison's analysis that World War II serves as a possible watershed. His statement, however, does not account for the large reduction in women pastoring between 1925 and 1930. While women may have experienced "more freedom and greater responsiblity," after World War I, the statistics indicate that fewer women were actually pastoring after 1930. Also, an editorial in the *Gospel Trumpet* by F.G. Smith documents an "antiwoman" attitude in the Church of God as early as 1920. Smith authored the editorial in response to a letter from a woman who had pastored a large church for several years. She was beginning to doubt if a woman should be in charge of an established congregation. Her doubts were generated by other ministers who were taking the position that women can preach and teach under certain conditions but should never be permitted to have charge of a settled church (Smith 1920, 2).

Factors influencing the reduction of women pastors come not only from the secular realm. A "fundamentalist leavening" also accounts for the anti-woman mentality, particularly in this generation. Churches and individuals who oppose women in ministry have promoted their opinions aggressively through the print medium and on television. Insisting on their literal interpretation of scripture, they accuse other churches that ordain women of being influenced by the current revival of the women's movement.

One of the values of this book is its reminder that the afffirmation of women is a strong component of the heritage of the Church of God. Biblical interpretations by Church of God writers throughout our history have counteracted literal approaches to Scripture intended to limit women's involvement in ministry.

The change in attitude concerning women pastors can also be attributed to the shift from a prophetic to a priestly understanding of authority in the church. While Charles Barfoot and Gerald Sheppard examined this change in several Pentecostal churches, their analysis is relevant to the Church of God as well. They document the dramatic decrease in the number of women clergy as their respective denominations experience "routinization" or the change from prophetic to priestly authority (Barfoot 1980).

(See Chapter 1 of this volume for a brief description of these understandings of authority. While this section of the appendix focuses on why the number of women clergy has declined, the aforementioned chapter stresses why the Church of God initially affirmed women in ministry.)

This brief analysis raises more questions than it offers answers. But once we ask the questions, we can begin searching for the answers. It is easier to offer broad generalizations than to pinpoint why decline occurred at a specific time. Following are several questions that deserve further exploration:

1. What are the statistics on women in staff positions? How do they compare with figures on men in staff positions?

2. How is the experience of black women pastors the same or different from white women?

3. Did all women evangelists become pastors? Document the shift from a flying ministry to a settled ministry.

4. How much did the eschatological emphasis influence the role of women initially and now?

5. What was the role of male leaders in the Church of God who opposed the ministry of women? Did specific men in the era from 1925-1935 limit the accessibility of women to pastoral positions?

These tentative observations are intended to suggest areas needing further investigation.

---

*Data for 1930, 1980, and 1985 has been added. All data is taken from the *Yearbook of the Church of God.*
**See Sharon Sawyer 1976 for information about women pastors in the Church of God.

Appendix D

Pastoral Placement Data, 1989**

200 Congregations open to pastoral placement as of January
18, 1989
Largest Number: 21 Ohio, 15 Kentucky, 11 Indiana
182 Available ministers requesting assistance in placement
 69 Associates

During 1988

145 Ordained: 123 Male, 23 Female

104 White	23 Youngest
31 Black	87 Oldest
2 Hispanic	39 Average

11 Anderson University
12 Mid-America Bible College
 3 Warner Pacific College
 7 Warner Southern College
43 Other
76/145*
20 Anderson University School of Theology
8 Other
28/145*

*Approximately 1/2 of our ordinards are college grads; 1/5
seminary grads
**Source Keith Huttenlocker
   Division of Church Service

ANNOTATED BIBLIOGRAPHY

Abbreviations to frequently cited sources:

GT   *Gospel Trumpet*

Quest   Smith, John W. V. 1980. *Quest for Holiness and Unity.* Anderson, Ind.: Warner Press.

Herald Smith, John W.V. 1955. *Herald of a Brighter Day.* Anderson, Ind.: Gospel Trumpet Company.

Passport Crose, Lester. 1983. *Passport for a Reformation.* Anderson, Ind.: Warner Press.

Allison, Joseph. 1974. "The Life of D.S. Warner: Singing His Praises." *Vital Christianity,* Anderson, Ind.: Warner Press. Dec. 1, 13.

———— 1976. "Heroines of the Faith." *Vital Christianity.* May 2, 12. See also *Quest* 165.

———— 1978. "An Overview of the Involvement of Women in the Church of God from 1916." *The Role of Women in Today's World.* Anderson, Ind.: Commission on Social Concerns, Church of God.

———— 1988. "Why We Encourage Women to Be Leaders." *Church of God Missions.* Anderson, Ind.: Missions Education Committee. January.

Anderson, Sara Joneane. 1980. "A Study of Leadership Roles of Six Selected Ordained Women in the Church of God in Anderson, Indiana." June. Thesis submitted to the Faculty of the School of Theology in partial fulfillment of the requirements for the degree of Master of Arts in Religion.

Aristotle. 1932. *Politics I.* 1253b 7-8; 1254a 22-23, 29-31; 1254b 13-21, emphasis added; trans. H. Rackham. Loeb Classical Library. New York: G.P. Putnam's Sons.

Aristotle. 1956. *Nicomachean Ethics V.* 1134b 9-18. Trans. H. Rackham. LCL. Cambridge: Harvard University. In the same writing Aristotle assumes that since the one owned is "as it were a part of oneself and no one chooses to harm himself; hence there can be no injustice towards them and nothing just or unjust in the political sense." He was advocating a benign tyranny based on inferior/superior natures. Yet, the Roman stoic Seneca critiqued Roman treatment of slaves as "excessively haughty, cruel and insulting." Senaca. *Moral Epistles,* 47.1 and 11, trans. Richard M. Gummere. LCL. New York: G.P. Putnam's Sons, 1917.

Balch, David L. 1981. *Let Wives be Submissive: The Domestic Code in 1 Peter.* The Society of Biblical Literature Monograph Series, 26. Chicago: Scholars Press, 161-173.

――― 1984. "Early Christian Criticism of Patriarchal Authority: 1 Peter 2:11—3:12." *Union Seminary Quarterly Review,* 39:3. A discussion of Aristotelian political philosophy is found in this essay. The table on 161 expresses the household codes. This layout of the passage also reveals the qualification of each aspect of the code. I am indebted to Balch's summary of Harnack's work. *See also* Harnack 1908 and Buchanan 1958.

――― 1986. "Hellenization/Acculturation in 1 Peter," *Perspectives on First Peter.* Charles H. Talbert, ed. Macon, Ga.: Mercer University Press, 79-102. I agree with Balch on the meaning of the household codes in the text of 1 Peter as I have presented it in this paper. For the source of much of this discussion see Balch 1984.

Barfoot, Charles H. and Gerald T. Sheppard. 1980. "Prophetic Vs. Priestly Religion: The Changing Role of Women Clergy in Classical Pentecostal Churches." *Review of Religious Research.* September, 2-17.

Bargerstock, Ilene, ed. 1988. *1988 Yearbook of the Church of God United States and Canada.* Anderson, Ind. Executive Council of the Church of God. Division of World Service.

Barrett, C.K. 1968. *The First Epistle to the Corinthians.* Harper's New Testament Commentaries. New York: Harper and Row.

Beverly, Sethard. 1988. Telephone interview with Mary Frambo's great-grandson, Sethard Beverly of Kansas City, Kans. December 20.

Bewer, Julius A. 1911. *The International Critical Commentaries: Obadiah and Joel.* New York: Scribner's Sons.

Biographical sketch n.d. Written for the Women of the Church of God program materials. Author not identified.

Bishop, Sarah. n.d. "Should Women Preach?" Gospel Trumpet Company. May 27, 9. Galatians 3:28 is employed in defense of women's ministries.

Bowers, Joyce M. 1984. "Roles of Married Women Missionaries: a Case Study." *International Bulletin of Missionary Research.* January.

Brayer, M. Menachem. 1986. *The Jewish Woman in Rabbinic Literature: A Psychosocial Perspective.* Vol. I. Hoboken, New York: KTAV Publishing House, Inc.

_____ 1986. *The Jewish Woman in Rabbinic Literature: A Psychohistorical Perspective.* Vol. II, Chapter 3. Hoboken, N.Y.: KTAV Publishing House.

Brown, C.E. 1939. "Women Preachers." Anderson, Ind.: Gospel Trumpet Company. May 27, 5, 13. Galatians 3:28 is employed in defense of women's ministries.

_____ 1951. *When the Trumpet Sounds.* Anderson, Ind.: Gospel Trumpet Company.

Bruce, F.F. 1982. *The Epistle to the Galatians.* The New International Greek Testament Commentary. Grand Rapids, Mich.: Wm. B. Eerdmans.

Buchanan, Neil, 1958. *History of Dogma.* New York: Russell and Russell. I, 45-57, 116-128; II, 169, 174.

Byers, A.L. 1920. "Pioneers of the Present Reformation: Sketch No. 3—Mary Cole." Gospel Trumpet Company, Feb. 19, 23.

_____ 1920. "Pioneers of the Present Reformation: Sketch No. 5—G.T. Clayton," Gospel Trumpet Company, March 4, 9.

———— 1920. "Pioneers of the Present Reformation: N. 12—Lodema Kaser." Gospel Trumpet Co., April 22, 5-6.

———— 1921. *The Birth of a Reformation or the Life and Labors of Daniel S. Warner.* Anderson, Ind.: Gospel Trumpet Company, 354.

Caldwell, Dondeena. 1988. "The Single Woman's Contribution to Missions." *Church of God Missions.* March, 5-8.

———— 1988. "Missionary? Wife? or Both?" *Church of God Missions.* March, 8.

Callen, Barry L. 1971. "Women in Ministry." Unpublished paper for Dialogue on Women in Ministry. February 10.

Carroll, Jackson W. 1982. Barbara W. Hargrove, Adair T. Lummis. "Women of the Cloth." *Grapevine.* November, 2.

Cassius, Dio. 1917. *Roman History.* 50.25.3 and 28.3. Trans. Ernest Cary. LCL. New York: G.P. Putnam's Sons.

Catholic Biblical Association's Committee on the Role of Women. 1979. "Women and Priestly Ministry: The New Testament Evidence." Catholic Biblical Quarterly 41: 609, 613.

Childress, James F. and Macquarrie, John, eds. 1986. *The Westminster Dictionary of Christian Ethics.* Philadelphia: Westminster Press.

Church of God in Black Perspective. 1970. Proceedings of the Caucus of Black Churchmen in the Church of God. Cleveland, Ohio: Shining Light Survey Press, April.

Clarke, Adam. n.d. *The Holy Bible . . . with a Commentary and Critical Notes.* 6 Vols. New York: Abingdon 3:342.

Clear, Valoris B. 1977. *Where the Saints Have Trod: A Social History of the Church of God Reformation Movement.* Chesterfield, Ind.: Midwest Publications.

Cole, George L. n.d. "The Labor of Women in the Gospel," 1.

———— 1900. In Wickersham, Henry C. *A History of the Church.* Moundsville, W.Va. Gospel Trumpet Co.

Cole, Mary. 1914. *Trials and Triumphs of Faith.* Anderson, Ind.: Gospel Trumpet Company.

Davis, Katie M. 1985. *Zion's Hill at West Middlesex.* Corpus Christi, Tex.: Christian Triumph Press, first pub. 1917.

Douglas, J.D., ed. 1982. *New Bible Dictionary Second Edition.* Wheaton, Ill.: Tyndale House Publishers.

Downer, Hattie. "Ivory Downer: Doer of Dreams." *Church of God Missions* magazine. Vol. 37. January, No. 5.

Dulin, Robert O. "Pansy Brown: Commitment Makes Christian Stateswoman." *Christian Leadership.* Vol. 35. No. 6. June, 10.

Eculink. 1988. "Women Clergy Double in Decade." September. Contains statistical data for decline in women clergy.

Elliot, John H. 1981. *A Home for the Homeless: A Sociological Exegesis of 1 Peter, its Solution and Strategy.* Philadelphia: Fortress Press. *See also* David L. Balch 1981. The articles most helpful for the argument developed here concerning the household codes are by these same two scholars: *see also* Elliott 1986 and Balch 1986.

———— 1986. "1 Peter, Its Situation and Strategy: A Discussion with David Balch." *Perspectives on First Peter.* Charles H. Talbert, ed. Macon, Ga.: Mercer University Press, 61-78.

Engstrom, Ted. W. 1988. Edward R. Dayton. "The Best Man for the Job." *World Vision.* June-July, 15.

"Fields are White, Laborers are Few." 1988. *Michigan Assembly of Church of God Newsletter.* East Lansing, Mich. December.

Froese, Walter. 1980. "John Wesley and Christian Holiness." *Centering on Ministry.* Anderson, Ind.: School of Theology, Anderson University. Winter. Vol. 5. No. 2.

Garcia, Gloria Salazar de. 1987. "Women's Ministries." *Latin American Pastoral Issues.* December.

Godbey, William. 1891. *Woman Preachers.* Atlanta Ga.: Office of the Way of Life.

Grubbs, Jerry. 1988. A fifteen-year study on the trends of ministerial leadership.

G.T. (Gospel Trumpet.) 1894. "News from the Field." December 27, 3.

———— 1908. "Mother Smith Goes to Rest." March 12, 8.

———— 1898. March 3, 5.

Hale, Mabel. n.d. "History of the Beginning and Early Years of the Church of God in Oklahoma City, Okla." Anderson, Ind.: School of Theology Library, Anderson University.

Hardesty, Nancy A. 1984. *Women Called to Witness Evangelical Feminism in the 19th Century.* Nashville: Abingdon Press.

————, Lucille Sider Dayton and Donald W. Dayton. 1979. "Women in the Holiness Movement: Feminism in the Evangelical Tradition" in *Women of Spirit: Female Leadership in the Jewish and Christian Traditions.* Edited by Rosemary Reuther and Eleanor McLaughlin. New York: Simon and Schuster, 225-254.

Harkness, Georgia. 1972. *Women in Church and Society.* Nashville: Abingdon Press.

Harnack, Adolph von. 1908. *The Mission and Expansion of Christianity in the First Three Centuries.* James Moffatt, trans. New York: G.P. Putnam's Sons. I, 19,31,77,314. *See also* Balch 1981, 84 for a summary of Harnack's work and Buchanan 1958.

———— 1958. *History of Dogma.* Trans. Neil Buchanan. New York: Russell and Russell.

Havelock, Ronald G. 1973. *The Change Agent's Guide to Innovation in Education.* Educational Technology Publications. Englewood Cliff, N.J.

Herald. See abbreviations at beginning of Annotated Bibliography for frequently cited works.

Hestenes, Roberta. 1988. "Is the Gospel Good News for Women?" *World Vision.* June/July, 11.

Hiebert, Paul. 1986. Phenomenology and Institutions: Syllabus and Lecture Outlines. Pasadena: Fuller Theological Seminary.

Hiscox, Edward. 1906. The Star Book for Ministers. Philadelphia: Judson Press.

Hooker, M.D. n.d. *New Testament Studies.* x, 410-416. Deals with authority as used in Paul's writings.

Jeremias, Joachim. 1949. *Jerusalem in the Time of Jesus.* Philadelphia: Fortress Press. Rabbi Eliezer ben Hyrkanos is credited with the quotation that burning the Torah is better than teaching it to a woman (373). "The right to divorce was exclusively the husband's." Public stigma and the requirement that the financial agreement in the marriage contract be honored, and the money returned, acted as a deterrent for hasty divorce. Therefore, the Hillelite provision for capricious divorce was not necessarily fulfilled. This issue does expose the attitudes of the day, however (370).

Jewett, Paul K. 1975. *Man as Male and Female.* Grand Rapids, Mich.: Wm. B. Eerdmans. First Addendum: Misogyny in Western Thought, 149-159. Not long after the New Testament era misogynism developed in full form both in Jewish and Christian literature. Aristotle's low evaluation of women is well documented and the Greek culture certainly influenced these times. The Jewish law that a woman was unclean during menstruation (Leviticus 15:19ff) and the rabbinical speculations on the special culpability of woman in the Fall were developed into negative doctrines and attitudes by some early church fathers.

———— 1980. *The Ordination of Women.* Grand Rapids, Mich.: Wm. B. Eerdmans Publishing Co.

Jordan, Wilfred. 1981. "Commemorative Booklet for the National Association of the Church of God."

Lanchester, H.C.O. et al. 1915. *Joel and Amos.* S.R. Driver, Ed. Cambridge, Mass.: The University Press.

LaTourette, Kenneth S. 1943. *History of the Expansion of Christianity.* Vol. 2. New York: Harper and Brothers.

Lee, Luther. 1975. "Women's Right to Preach the Gospel." *Five Sermons and a Tract.* Ed. Donald W. Dayton. Chicago: Holrad House, 88-91.

Leonard Juanita E. 1965. "The Social Work Agency: An Arm of the Church." *Christian Leadership.* Board of Christian Education of the Church of God. October. Vol. 20. No. 10.

Loveland, Anne C. 1977. "Domesticity and Religion in the Antebellum Period: The Career of Phoebe Palmer." *Historian.* May, 259, 261. *See also* Stanley 1987; Wickersham 1900 for Sarah Smith and Alma White, other sanctified women whose timidity transformed into holy boldness.

Maines, Carole. 1983. "Missionary Wives: Underused Asset." *Evangelical Missions Quarterly.* October, 295.

Malcomb, Kari Torjesen. 1982. *Women at the Crossroads: A Path Beyond Feminism and Traditionalism.* Downers Grove, Ill.: InterVarsity Press.

Martin, Ralph P. 1984. *The Spirit and the Congregation.* Grand Rapids, Mich.: Wm. B. Eerdmans. The summary and critique of a number of these attempts to explain the apparent inconsistency is most helpful.

_____ 1986. Graduate lecture on 1 Peter. Fuller Theological Seminary. Spring quarter. Martin thinks household codes are better defined as station codes in 1 Peter. His reasoning is that the area to which the letter is addressed is an outpost of the Roman Empire and that classical thinking is less developed here. The letter, however, was probably written from Rome, the center of such classical thinking. Also, Alexander the Great (a student of Aristotle) had campaigned three centuries earlier to Hellenize his empire. Consequently Hellenization would have been integrated into the general culture by the New Testament era. In this way, Martin's conservatism must be tempered.

Massey, James Earl. 1957. *An Introduction to the Negro Churches in the Church of God Reformation Movement.* New York: Shining Light Survey Press.

McCutcheon, Lillie. 1980. "Lady in the Pulpit." *Centering on Ministry.* Anderson, Ind.: The Center for Pastoral Studies. Winter, 5-6.

Mickelsen, Alvera, ed. 1986. *Women, Authority, and the Bible.* Downers Grove, Ill.: InterVarsity Press. Susie Stanley. "Galatians 3:28 Response," 179-186. Gives further information on the use of Galatians 3:28 to support women preachers.

Morgan, Marcus H. 1951. "The Negro Church of God." Unpublished paper. Anderson, Ind.: Anderson University. May 21, 7.

Pagels, Elaine H. 1974. "Paul and Women: A Response to Recent Discussion." AAR annual meeting presentation, Chicago, 546. This language is created by Pagels as an attempt to recognize the motivations for various teachings on women.

Palmer, Phoebe 1859. *The Promise of the Father: or, A Neglected Speciality of the Last Days.* Boston: Henry V. Degen. Reprinted ed. Salem, Ohio: Schmul Publishers n.d., See also Hardesty 1984, White 1986, and Kaser 1987.

Passport. See abbreviations at beginning of Annotated Bibliography for frequently cited works.

Phillips, Harold. 1978. "The Church in Her House." *Vital Christianity.* May 7.

Phillips, J.B, trans. 1962. *The New Testament in Modern English.* New York: MacMillan.

Plutarch 1928. *Advice to Bride and Groom.* 140D and 140DE, trans. Frank Cole Babbitt. LCL. New York: G.P. Putnam's Sons.

Quest. See abbreviations at beginning of Annotated Bibliography for frequently cited works.

Randall, Naomi. n.d. *Naomi Randall's Diary.* Anderson, Ind.: Archives of the Board of Church Extension and Home Missions of the Church of God.

Raser, Harold E. 1987. *Phoebe Palmer: Her Life and Thought.* Lewiston, New York: The Edwin Mellen Press. See also White 1986 for another recent biography of Phoebe Palmer.

Roberts, Benjamin T. 1891. *Ordaining Women.* Rochester, N.Y.: Earnest Christian Publishing House, 55.

Rogers, Everett M., Shoemaker, Floyd F. 1976. *Communication of Innovations: A Cross Cultural Approach.* Second Edition. New York, London: Free Press MacMillan.

Ruether, Rosemary Radford and Skinner, Rosemary Keller, eds. 1986. *Women and Religion in America.* Vol. 3. San Francisco: Harper and Row.

Sawyer, Sharon. 1976. "Women Pastors in the Church of God." *Colloquium.* July/August. Vol. 8. Number 4.

———— 1988. "Findings: Women Clergy Double in a Decade." *Eculink.* September, no. 20.

———— 1984. "Directions toward the Year 2,000." Report of 1984 Consultation on Mission and Ministry. Committee on Long Range Planning. Anderson, Ind.: Executive Council of the Church of God.

Schaller, Lyle E. 1972. *The Change Agent: the Strategy of Innovative Leadership.* Nashville: Abingdon Press.

Scholer, David M. 1984. "Women in Ministry." *The Covenant Companion.* December 1983-February 1984. As many commentators have recognized, Paul's term for *authority* includes the sense of active exercise (and not passive reception of it as some have claimed) See. p. 17. *See also* Barrett, 1968, 253-4 and M.D. Hooker n.d., *New Testament Studies.* x, 410-416.

Seneca. 1917. *Moral Epistles* 47. Trans. Richard M. Gummere. Loeb Classical Library. New York: G.P. Putnam's Sons.

Shoffner, Lena. 1900. From Wickersham, *A History of the Church.* Moundsville, W.Va.: Gospel Trumpet Co., 336.

Smith, F.G. 1920. "Editorial." *Gospel Trumpet.* October 14, 2.

———— 1920. *Gospel Trumpet,* October 14.

Smith, Fred. 1984. *You and Your Network.* Waco: Word Books.

Smith, J.M. Powis et.al. 1911. *The International Critical Commentary Series: Micah, Zephaniah, Nahum, Habbakkuk, Obadiah, and Joel.* New York: Scribner's Sons.

Smith, John W.V. Smith. 1955. See abbreviations at beginning of annotated bibliography for frequently cited works.

_____ 1985. *I Will Build My Church.* Anderson, Ind.: Warner Press.

Smith, Sarah. 1892. "Fifty Years in the Kingdom of Heaven." *Gospel Trumpet.* Jan 21, n.p.

_____ 1900. "Autobiography." In Wickersham, Henry C., *A History of the Church.* Moundsville, W.Va.: Gospel Trumpet Co.

_____ 1902. *Life Sketches of Mother Sarah Smith.* Anderson, Ind.: Gospel Trumpet Company.

Stanley, Susan. 1987. "Alma White: Holiness Preacher with a Feminist Message." Ph.D. dissertation, Iliff School of Theology, University of Denver, 46, 48, 51. See 304-329 for a summary of Scriptural arguments used in the Holiness Movement to support women preachers.

See also Loveland 1977 and Wickersham 1900 for Phoebe Palmer and Sarah Smith, other sanctified women whose timidity transformed into holy boldness.

_____ 1986. "Galatians 3:28 Response." In *Women, Authority, and the Bible.* Alvera Mickelsen, ed. Downer's Grove, Ill.: InterVarsity Press, 179-186. Further information on Galatians 3:28 to support women preachers.

Stendahl, Kristen. 1966. *The Bible and the Role of Women.* Trans. by Emilie T. Sander. Philadelphia: Fortress Press. Pacet Books, Biblical Series 15.1.

Stern, Rabbi 1928. *Daily Prayers,* New York: Hebrew Publishing. This prayer of thanks for not being a woman occurs in this popular volume. It remains part of the orthodox Jewish expression today. The earliest record identified thus far for this prayer is in the work of Rabbi Judah ben Elai, c. A.D. 150. But the formula itself can be traced back to the Greek Thales who was grateful that he was a man and not a beast, a man and not a woman, and a Greek and not a barbarian. (Diog. Laert., Vit. Phil. 1.33.) Socrates said substantially the same thing and Aristotle adopted his thinking. As noted earlier, Alexander the Great spread Aristotle's teachings by Hellenization in the 300s B.C. His empire covered much of what would later become the Roman Empire. (See expanded argument in Bruce 1982.)

Telfer, David. 1972. *Red & Yellow Black & White & Brown.* Anderson, Ind.: Warner Press, 48.

Thompson, John A. 1956. *The Interpreter's Bible: The Book of Joel.* Vol. 6. New York, Nashville: Abingdon Press.

Tucker, Ruth A., Liefeld, Walter. 1987. *Daughters of the Church: Women and Ministry from New Testament Times to the Present.* Grand Rapids, Mich.: Academic Books, Zondervan.

Wattleton, Ozie G. 1988. Telephone interview. Atlanta, Georgia, December 20.

Watts, John D. 1975. *The Cambridge Bible: The Books of Joel, Obadiah, Jonah, Nahum, Habakkuk, and Zephaniah.* New York: Cambridge University Press.

White, Alma. 1921. *Woman's Ministry.* London: Pillar of Fire.

———— 1935-1943. *The Story of My Life and Pillar of Fire.* Zarephath, N.J.: Pillar of Fire. See 3:360 for an example of the woman of Samaria illustrating God's approval of women's ministry.

White, Charles. 1986. *The Beauty of Holiness.* Grand Rapids, Mich.: Francis Asbury Press of Zondervan Publishing House. *See also* Raser 1987 for another recent biography of Phoebe Palmer.

Wickersham, Henry C. 1900. "Autobiography." *A History of the Church.* Moundsville, W.Va.: Gospel Trumpet Company. *See also* Loveland 1977 and Stanley 1987 for Phoebe Palmer and Alma White, other sanctified women whose timidity transformed into holy boldness.

Wilson, Bryan R. 1970. *Religious Sects.* New York: McGraw-Hill, 59-60.

Williams, Hans Walter. 1974. *Anthropology of the Old Testament.* Philadelphia: Fortress Press.

Williams, Lima Lehmer. 1986. *Walking in Missionary Shoes.* Anderson, Ind.: Warner Press, 99.

Wolff, Hans Walter. 1974. *Anthropology of the New Testament.* Philadelphia: Fortress Press. *Cf.* Jewett 1975, 123-128.

For Further Reading

Fischer, Kathleen. *Women at the Well.* New York: Paulist Press, 1988.

Hardesty, Nancy. *Women Called to Witness.* Nashville: Abingdon Press, 1984.

Hassey, Janette. *No Time for Silence: Evangelical Women in Public Ministry Around the Turn of the Century.* Grand Rapids, Mich.: Academic Books, Zondervan, 1986.

Hull, Gretchen Gaebelein. *Equal to Serve: Women and Men in the Church and Home.* Old Tappan, N.J.: Revell, 1987.

Longenecker, Richard N. *New Testament Social Ethics for Today.* Grand Rapids, Mich.: Eerdmans, 1984.

Mickelsen, Alvera, Ed. *Women, Authority & the Bible.* Downers Grove, Ill.: InterVarsity Press, 1986.

Rhodes, Lynn N. *Co-Creating: A Feminist Vision of Ministry.* Philadelphia: The Westminster Press, 1987.

Russell, Letty M. *Household of Freedom.* Philadelphia: The Westminster Press, 1987.

Swartley, Willard. *Slavery, Sabbath, War and Women.* Scottdale, Pa.: Herald Press, 1983.

Tucker, Ruth and Liefeld, Walter. *Daughters of the Church.* Grand Rapids, Mich.: Zondervan, 1987.

Weidman, Judith, ed. *Women Ministers: How Women Are Redefining Traditional Roles.* New York: Harper and Row, 1985.

Index

A

Acts 1
African Assembly 85
Alexander, Katie 59
Allan, Naomi 85
Allison, Joseph 176, 177
American Bible Society 81
American Indian Council 98
Anderson, Evelyn Janes 72
Anderson, Noel 72
Anderson, Pearlie 124
Anderson Bible Training School xiv
Anglican Hospital 92
Anna 8, 40
Apphia 9
Aristotle 5, 23, 28
Ashenfelter, Mabel 54
Assemblies of God 159
Attributes of God 133
Authority/subordination model 23
Ayala, Tito 79

B

Babb, Yvonne 65
Bailey, Esther 97
Bailey, George 82
Bailey, Ivory, Jr. 124
Bailey, Mrs. (George) 82
Baker, Mabel 81, 84, 85
Balch, David 23 ff.
Barfoot, Charles 178
Barge, Curtis 122, 125

Barrett, C. K. 20
Barrow, Willie Taplin 63
Beach, Verda 65
Bean, Juanita 96
Berthelsen, Mary 71
Bishop, Sarah 38
Bolds, Sister 49
Borden, Norma 94
Bowen, Lloyd 124
Brayer, M. Menachem 6
Brewster, Violet 68
Bridges, Johanna 155
Brown, Pansy Melvina Major 65
Bryant, S. G. 51
Bugg, Andrew 122
Butz, Mary 95

C

Caldwell, Dondeena 95
California Conference on Child Health and Protection 52
Callen, Barry 155, 159, 164
Callita, Sister 70
Carmen, Sister Hermana 70
Children's Home 51
Christian Triumph Company 72
Church of the Nazarene 159
Civil Rights Movement 154
Clark, Frances 90
Clear, Valoris 152
Clown Horse, Ben 97
Cole, George L. 38, 50
Cole, Jeremiah 48
Cole, Mary 36, 40, 41, 45, 47, 48, 49, 50, 51
Coleman, Agnes 63
Commission on Social Concerns 156, 157
Committee on Long-range Planning xiv
Concilio 77
Conkis, Mrs. (William) 83

Consultation of 1984 xv
Consultation on Women in Ministry and Mission xv, 160
Cooper, Lena 59
Cotto, David 77
Cotto, Tina 77
Critser, Kay 89, 96
Crose, Lester 94
Crosswhite, Joseph 60
Crosswhite, Mother Emma Alberta Nelson 59, 60, 61
Cumberbatch, Theodosia 65
Curry, Willie 116
Curtis, James H. 113

D

Dallas, Mrs. (George) 83
Day of Pentecost 2, 14
Davila, Gilberto 76, 78
Davis, Katie 59
Dean, Bernie 94
Deborah 8, 40
Division of Church Service 157
Dominance/subordination 29
Dominguez, Rosita 79
Donohew, Grace 95
Downer, Early 61
Downer, Hattie 62, 77, 79
Dunn, S. P. 117

E

Eculink 42
Elliott, John 23
Engst, Irene 86
Engstrom, Ted 98
Esther 9
Euodia 9, 18
Executive Council of the Church of God xiv, 160

F

Farag, Marilyn 90
Finkbeiner, Mina 67
Finney, Charles G. 151
Fletcher, Mrs. 46
Floating Bethel 52
Flying ministries 45, 156
Foggs, Edward 156
Ford, Edward A. 62
Ford, Nancy McClure 62, 63
Frambo, Mary 58
Frazer, Wilhelmina 65, 86
Friends' Hospital 92

G

Garrett, Ozie 61
General Ministerial Assembly 91, 92, 156
Gerodetti, Sarah Tafolla 71
Godbey, William 39
Graeco-Roman culture, values 23, 28
Greer, Hester 65

H

Hale, Mable 55
Hall, Annie 63
Hall, Jewell 85, 86
Hanson, Lydia 86
Hardesty, Nancy 154
Harkness, Georgia 6, 7, 8, 84
Harnack, Adolph von 27
Harrison, Harold 77
Harrison, Jackie 77
Hawk, Ida 97
Hellenization process 28
Henry, L. E. 52

Henry, W. J. 52
Hestenes, Roberta 92
Hester, Juanita 114
High, Ellen 85
Hittle, Bessie 84
Holiness and unity 133
Holiness Movement 36, 40, 41
Hoops, Magaline 96
Household codes 23, 24, 26, 31, 33
Huldah 8, 40
Hunter, Clarence Edgar 52
Hunter, Nora Siens 36, 40, 51-54, 154, 176

J

Jael 8
James, Christine 59
Janes, Brother L. Y. 71, 72, 73
Janes, Sister L. Y. 71, 72
Janes, Una 72, 73
Jeremias, Joachim 15
Jarrett, Minna 153
Joel 3, 9, 10, 14, 18, 30
Joiner, Mrs. (Samuel) 83
Junia 19
Junias 19

K

Kaser, George 47
Kaser, Lodema 47, 50, 51
Kiger, Nannie 44
Kilmer, Ruth 94
Kilpatrick, Alexander J. 43
Kinley, Phyllis 93
Kramer, Gertrude 81
Kuna Indians 89
Kurrle, Tabita Meier 68

L

LaBuena Tierra Bible Institute (IBBT) 73
LaTourette, Kenneth 164
Lambe, Ruth Ann 65
Laughlin, Nellie 84
Lee, Luther 38
Lehmer, Lima 85
Lewis, Juanita 64
Lewis, Melinda 63
Lorton, George 60
Ludwig, John 85
Ludwig, Twyla 83, 85

M

Maciel, A. T. 73
Makokha, Byrum 95
Malcomb, Kari Torgensen 151
Mansfield, Cindy 75
Mansfield, Richard 75
Martin, George 82
Martin, Mrs. (George) 82
Martin, Ralph 21
Martin, Vera 86
Massey, Gwendolyn 65, 98
Matthesen, Ed 55
Matthesen, Lena Shoffner 36
McCrie, Josephine 84
McCutcheon, Lillie 96, 112, 153, 177
McManus, Nell 155
Medical Council of Kenya 86
Meier, Lillian 68
Meyer, Emma 153
Meyer, Marie 155
Middlebrooks, June Downing 113
Miller, Barbara 88, 92
Miller, Frances (Frankie) 44, 51
Ministerial Committee of Panama 68

Miriam 7, 40
Missionary homes 51, 52
Moore, Delores Anita 116
Moore, Evelyn Bernice 120
Moore, Frank 123
Moore, Vivian Radden 115, 128
Moors, Mona 85
Morgan, Marcus 60
Morgan, Mary 65
Mundul, Nolina 85
Mundul, Sonat 85
Murray, Ruth 81

N

National Assembly of the Church of God in Havana, Cuba 70
National Association of the Church of God 143
National Board of Church Extension and Homes Missions 98
National Consultation on Women in Ministry and Missions xiii
1984 Consultation on Mission and Ministries: Directions Toward the Year 2,000 xiv
Newell, Arlo 121
Nisely, Joyce 155
Noadiah 8
Nympha 9

O

Ogle, Edwin C. 113
Olson, Nellie 94

P

Palmer, Ellsworth 74
Palmer, Hilaria 74
Palmer, Phoebe 37, 38, 39 46, 151

Index

Parham, Agnes 127
Parham, Douglas 127
Parisi, Miriam 71
Parvey, Constance 159, 171
Patterson, D. W. 73
Paul 9, 10, 14, 18, 20, 21, 22, 27, 28, 30, 41
Pentecost 3, 30, 40
Peters, Edith 68
Peters, Elizabeth 59
Perez-Scrivner, Cati 75
Philemon 9
Phillips, Harold 177
Phoebe 9, 18, 21, 41
Plutarch 26
Priscilla 9, 18, 21, 33
Pye, George 82
Pye, Mrs. (George) 82

R

Radden, Delores Anita 116
Radden, James C. 116
Radden, Thomas 116
Randall, Naomi 97
Ratzlaff, Nina 94
Reedy, Edward 82
Reedy, Mrs. (Edward) 82
Ricketts, Amanda 65
Rivas, Claudina Ocasio de 70
Roaché, Sylvia 65
Roberts, B. T. 39, 40
Rogers, Fern Ludwig 95
Rogers, Hester Ann 46
Romero, Carmen Martinez 70
Rupert, John 82
Rupert, Mrs. (John) 82

S

Samuels, Miriam 71
Sanders, Cheryl 65
Sanderson, Ruth 92
Sapp, Beatrice 63
Sawyer, Sharon 152, 176
Sawyer, Sheila 65
Schaffler, Dale 126
Schaller, Lyle 164
Schneider, Velma 86
Schwieger, Jenny 89
Sharp, Dorothy 96
Sheppard, Gerald 178
Shively, Kay 155
Shoffner, Lena 52, 53, 84
Shotton, Ruth 83, 88
Shultz, Retha 89, 92, 95
Siens, Nora 51
Smith, Ann 94, 98
Smith, Birdie 51, 84, 153
Smith, F. G. 37, 40, 51, 84, 177
Smith, Ivory Virginia 61, 62
Smith, J. Edgar 73
Smith, Mother Sarah Sauer 36, 39, 42, 43, 44, 45, 48
Smith, Ruth M. 102
Smith, S. J. 51
Smith, William 51
Snowden, Nellie J. 155
Spanish Concilio 98
Springer, Mrs. (Robert) 82
Springer, Robert 82
Spruell, Juanita 117
Stafford, Gilbert 158

Strickland, June D. 109
Swoope, Diana 65
Syntyche 9, 18

T

Tafolla, Annie 71
Taylor, Daisy 68, 69
Taylor, J. M. 127
Taylor, Mendoza 69
Taylor, Sarah 64
Thimes, Edna 86, 92
Tiesel, Margaret 94

U

Unity and holiness 137
Upham, Phoebe 151

V

Vanderlaan, Ken 124
Vazquez, Amelia Valdez 73
Vazquez, Iamuel 74
Villarreal, Aggie 78
Villarreal, Ana 78
Villarreal, John 78

W

Walker, Polly 58
Walls, Mary Lou 90
Warner, Daniel Sidney 43, 44, 48, 51, 53, 58, 151
Warren, Barney 44
Wattleton, Ozie Garrett 61
Wesley, John 37, 46, 151
Wesleyan Church 159
Wesleyan Holiness Movement 36, 37, 39, 41

Whalen, Emmitt 121
White, Alma 39, 40
Williams, Jane 58
Williams, Marge 97
Williams, (Reverend) 120
Wilson, Evelyn 65
Wimbish, Priscilla 59
Winston, Beatrice 116
Women in the Early Church 17
Women of the Church of God xv, 51, 53, 91, 155, 156, 157, 160
Women's Home and Foreign Missionary Society 53
Women's Missionary Society 53, 155
Wyatt, Addie 64

Y

Young, Edith 85
Yutzy, Glenna 96